Stories of Celebrating Divorce in your 20s

JOELLE CAPUTA

ISBN: 1499664370
ISBN 13: 9781499664379
Library of Congress Control Number: 2014910215
CreateSpace Independent Publishing Platform
North Charleston, South Carolina

Disclaimer: Certain participant and character names and locations have been changed.

To my happily ever after: Frank, Genevieve and our growing family, fur-kids included.

In loving memory of Skye Blue.

Contents

Introduction

Breaking Up is Hard to Do, But Worth it

<u>My Divorcée Demographics:</u>
Met future ex-husband: Age 25
Bling, bling, got the ring: Age 26
Got hitched: Age 27
Ditched: Age 28

I cut up my wedding dress. The $1,600 exquisite ivory, intricately floral beaded, drop-waist, sweetheart neckline, designer gown that I wore on what was supposed to be the happiest day of my life; the day I planned as the gateway to my happily ever after. I sliced into it with scissors and ripped it apart with my bare hands, performing my own open-heart surgery.

My wedding dress had become a haunting reminder that I was a 28-year-old divorcée. What was once considered a symbol of my future became a sparkling announcement of my failure.

How did I, a girl who chased her dreams and fantasized about falling in love and making babies with Mr. Right, end up on the verge of going bankrupt as a result of supporting a husband who quit multiple jobs, grew a beard on purpose because he knew she hated it and wouldn't kiss him as long as it existed, and had firmly decided he didn't want to be married—perhaps not to anyone, but definitely not to her—or ever have children?

Granted, our marital knot began to unravel shortly after we crossed the threshold as husband and wife. But, as someone who never gives up, I tried my hardest to honor my "for better or for worse" vows. When my then-husband told me he wanted to end our marriage, I was relieved. I did, too. We were both miserable.

Then, panic struck.

No twenty-something woman actually pictures herself divorced when all her friends are becoming brides and birthing babies. At that point, my own biological clock had sped up to the point that the hands were about to go flying off! The idea of starting over conjured worries about being too old to get pregnant by the time I picked up the pieces. I suffered insomnia-induced anxiety attacks and even hid in my bedroom during my first post-divorce holiday season to avoid the embarrassment of facing my extended family.

Eventually, I decided to stop agonizing over my potential future and focus on the present. During this time, I could have removed the matching "XO" tattoo my ex-husband and I got on our first (and only) wedding anniversary, decided it was the perfect time to break my life-long straight-edge lifestyle and start drinking, and driven my friends insane with weepy phone calls every five minutes.

Instead, I celebrated my divorce by setting and reaching goals and partaking in rituals—including trashing my dress, writing a good riddance list and compiling a dating checklist. Along the way, I even met the real Mr. Right.

When my marriage first ended, I couldn't find any divorce books to which I could relate. There were books from therapists filled with marriage-saving strategies and books with stories from suddenly single mothers who spent decades as wives. I didn't want to save my marriage so that nixed the majority of books on the shelves. Although I did read one collection of divorce stories, I found it difficult to relate to women who had children my age.

I discovered there was no literary representation for younger women who have courageously decided to end their marriages and just needed some reassurance that everything would be OK. I didn't just survive my divorce; I rocked it. And writing a book has always been one of my goals (I grew up writing stories on typewriters, remember those? I even cut models out of magazines and glued them onto the pages as characters). When I divorced, I naturally channeled my journalistic background and made it my mission to connect with others to let them know that not only is there life after divorce in your 20s, but life is indeed beautiful.

During the process, I discovered I'm not the lone wolf—I have a pack! By conducting interviews for this book and moderating discussions among divorced women currently in their 20s and early 30s who are members of my *Trash the Dress* private online support group, I've learned why twenty-something women are getting married and divorced and more importantly, how they are moving on from marriage.

From traveling with girlfriends and hosting divorce parties to raising money for local domestic violence shelters through 5k races, twenty-something divorcées are inspiring forces. United by this project, our celebration stories will pave the way for those whose lives are just turning down this winding road.

Before I trashed my dress, I thought I wasted the most important years of my life with my ex-husband. But while tearing the fabric of my wedding dress with clenched fists, I cleansed all of my self-loathing for marrying a man I wasn't 100 percent sure was "the one," but rather hoped would evolve into my perfect partner after we became husband and wife. Now, I'm thankful for the venom.

The mid-mid-life crisis that followed my so-called marriage may have shattered my life as I knew it then, but not the life I was meant to live.

The women featured on the following pages have also raised their naked left ring fingers high and waved their past goodbye. We're proof that breaking up is hard to do, but worth it. And that there is indeed a happily ever after post-divorce!

One

Love Brews at the Café

I 've always viewed the glass as half-full, looked on the bright side and put my faith in fate and music. Growing up, I dissected lyrics to my favorite songs. Whenever life got me down, all I had to do was repeat some of those lyrics to myself and be on my merry way.

I believe there's a great plan for everyone and everything happens for a reason, even if it doesn't make sense at the time. When my marriage first ended, I was at rock bottom. However, I chose to dance in the dirt. Clarity—and my greater life plan—emerged from chaos, just like one of my favorite songs assured me. The church of rock 'n' roll has never steered me wrong.

I was not raised in a very religious environment. My family did not attend weekly mass, but my mother made sure my younger brother, Joey, and I attended religion classes in order to complete the mandatory Catholic sacraments, despite my protest.

The older I got, the more I detested these lessons. One year, I missed out on an entire season of watching *Beverly Hills, 90120* because group meetings took place on Wednesday nights during the exact hour my favorite television show aired. So I sat in class with a bunch of people I didn't know or care to know and put a fake smile on my face as the teacher asked the same thing to me during every attendance check: "Joelle? Do you know your name is French?" I informed him that I was aware and 100 percent Italian, named after my father, Joe. Then I drifted into my own world, where I have existed ever since.

Now, as I said, I didn't pay attention during those classes, so I can't tell you much about Catholicism. However, I memorized the "Hail Mary" and "Our Father" prayers, repeated them to myself every night before bed (in total obsessive compulsive disorder fashion because I have always been paranoid of bad things happening to those I loved) and decided that religion can be a bit too organized for my taste. Weekly mass is not for me, but I have nothing against those who are devout followers of any religion. I believe in God—in my own way and on my own terms—which are private and not every Sunday morning during a service where attendees are obligated to shake hands with strangers sitting in nearby pews and drink out of the same wine glass. Um, hello? Germfest!

I am also adamantly against marriage preparation programs. I don't believe a madly-in-love couple needs a stranger to approve or deny their decision to spend the rest of their lives together. We're adults. We make mature decisions. And when those mature decisions to marry turn out to have been the wrong decisions, well, there's always divorce!

Obviously, no young woman gets married with divorce as her Plan B. However, sometimes "'Til death do we part" becomes "Death unless we part!" I'm not talking about suicide per se, but rather the death of our souls. Being trapped in an unhealthy marriage can strip even the most vibrant woman down to a shadow of her former self, a dark reminder following her every move.

It happened to me. My marriage led me to become a depressed, stressed out woman who sat on her couch alone at night wondering how her life came to be the total opposite of everything she had always envisioned. But I let it continue in hopes that one day things would get better.

Then, one day, reality slapped me in the face. My husband told me he didn't want to be married any longer. I was about to become a statistic—a woman divorced before age 30! While many would view my soon-to-be social status as devastating (and believe me, it was) I knew getting divorced was the best decision, even though I felt as rare as an endangered species.

The road on which I was about to embark was treacherous. I had no clue how I was going to navigate my way and was unsure of where it would lead, but I agreed that we needed to end our marriage.

I had seen this event coming for a very long time. Ironically, I never imagined that when I met Max he would end up being my future husband, let alone future ex-husband.

Max walked into my life through finger-smudged glass doors at a coffee shop where I was working as a barista while trying to launch my self-published music magazine, *Planet Verge*, on a national level. Max wore a long, fur-rimmed black coat and sunglasses. Slicked back hair and a nose ring completed his rock star look.

Lightning struck.

I began referring to Max behind his back as "Dave Navarro," as I gushed over him to one of my coworkers and best friends, Penny. Max looked just like the Jane's Addiction guitarist, so it was a fitting nickname.

After that day, Penny would call me during her shifts to report when "Dave Navarro" would come in for his daily cup. Turns out, he was there a lot with his best friend, Sam.

One day, Max struck up a conversation. While talking, I learned that, *be still my heart*, he was a hair stylist! When he offered to give me an edgy new look, I immediately took him up on his offer.

Little did I know it would end up being a four-hour haircut. Yes, four hours. This was at the very beginning of Max's career and I was among his first clients. That, on top of his attention to detail, meant that I was stuck in a salon chair until every single strand of hair was in perfect place. It was draining, but I didn't mind because it gave us a chance to become acquainted. When the haircut was finally complete, I noted that it was unfortunate that I looked so great but had nowhere go make an impression. Max suggested we grab a bite at a nearby bistro, which happened to be my favorite.

At the restaurant, Max flipped through a music magazine I had with me and talked a lot about Scott Weiland. Max had a man crush on the Stone Temple Pilots frontman the way I had a girl crush on Tori Spelling. I didn't think too much about it until it was our fifth time hanging out and he had yet to make a move. Then, I wondered if he was interested in being more than friends with any girl. Come on, he was a hair stylist and wore black nail polish! And it's not like I was holding a "Do Not Enter" sign!

Finally, one night we were in my car listening to music as we always did and Max leaned over and kicked those doubts out of my mind as he said, "Come here, sweetheart." We kissed a little and then he rested his head on my lap, which was cute.

"I could get used to this," I thought to myself. Luckily, Max reflected my feelings.

To think, there was a time when I didn't even want anything to do with Max. I ignored his calls and literally crossed the street when I was saw him walking around town. This was because I couldn't figure out if he was interested in a serious relation-ship and I didn't want to dedicate my precious husband-hunting years to something that was not destined to go anywhere. But alas, he won me over a little more each time he visited me at work.

All those coffee grinds must have gone to my brain. For some reason, I only focused on a pixel of the big picture. Max loved rock 'n' roll, let me paint his nails black, watched my fa-vorite show, *General Hospital*, with me, and gave my friends and me amazing haircuts. Looking back, I realize he was Mr. Right-What-I-Needed-At-That-Time-Of-My-Life, but not Mr. Who-I-Need-For-The-Rest-Of-My-Life. While those qualities made him a great boyfriend, they weren't what I needed in a husband. Yet, he became mine.

Sometime during the latter six months of our first year as a couple, Max told me to buy a bridal magazine because I'd never know when I'd need it. We were at a convenience store at that moment and of course those words brought a rush of blood flowing through my veins. And thus, I fell down the rabbit hole and got lost in a world of couture dresses, centerpieces and favors.

We booked a wedding venue before an engagement took place. Mistake number one.

One day, Max and I were sitting in the backyard of the house I lived in with my mother and brother. We mentioned how we hoped to be married in one year. I finally had a better job, working for a small music company, and we had been joined at the hip for the past twelve months, so marriage was the next logical step.

"Then you better start looking at venues," advised my mother. "Places book up years ahead of time."

That lit a fire. Max had always talked about having our wedding at a country club in his town. We booked an appointment to see the venue. The setting was exactly where I pictured my dream wedding to take place. It boasted space for an outdoor garden ceremony, a smorgasbord cocktail hour under a tent and a modest sized ballroom with a terrace overlooking a golf course. It was a no brainer. My mother had her checkbook so we scheduled our wedding date right then: September 21st. It was the beginning of thousands of dollars from her life savings my mother would throw away on my failed marriage.

Though we had the venue booked, I made it clear to Max that I still expected an engagement ring and proper request for my hand. So, he went to his family's jeweler and made a few selections before taking me for final approval. I chose the ring that was his favorite, as well. It was a unique vintage-inspired band with tiny specks of diamonds and filigree. I couldn't wait to get it on my finger.

Max didn't seem to have as much enthusiasm for that moment as I did, or at least it felt that way from the lack of thought I felt he put into the proposal. The day he popped the question, I came home from work to find Max sitting on my bed reading a magazine. My eyes immediately went to the ring box placed beside him, which I pried open, only to find it was empty. Disappointed that he could play such a joke on me, I walked over to my dresser.

That's when Max knelt down beside me and placed the round, humble diamond on my finger as he asked me to be his wife.

It was heartfelt, but a part of me was hoping for a little more creativity in the proposal, especially because I already knew it was coming. To make things even more glamorous, he chose to do so on a day that I had let my hair air dry and wore knee-length, army print cut-offs and a white tank top. I always like to look my best and that was certainly not one of those days. But, of course I accepted with pure joy.

I took a shower, applied a ruby red, sparkly polish to my nails and had Max blow dry my hair before we went for a celebratory dinner to the restaurant where we had our first "date." I can't call it a proper date because he didn't pay for me. He actually accepted my money when I offered to cover my portion of the bill. That should've been my first sign to run.

I did run, though it was to the bridal boutique. I had my brain set on a gown from a Greek designer noted for his exotic style. I had fallen in love with a magazine ad of a vintage goddess in a corset bodice and split skirt, lying on her side, sexily looking up towards the heavens. I tore out that page and saved it for the day I would actually be able to purchase the gown.

However, a lot of time had passed from when I started perusing wedding magazines to when Max and I actually got engaged. By the time I went to my local dress shop, I was served devastating news. My dream dress was discontinued!

The consultant told me to come back in a few weeks, when the store would be holding a trunk show. That day, my mom and I arrived for my appointment and lo and behold, one of the front mannequins was dressed in my dream gown! Well, almost. I'd call it the fraternal twin sister of my dream dress. Whereas the gown of my dreams had a visibly ribbed corset and halter neckline, the displayed gown was strapless with underlying ribbing and had a scalloped, sweetheart neckline.

"Oh my God!," I exclaimed. "That's my dress!"

I rushed right up to the bridal consultant at the front desk and told her I needed to try on that dress. She told me to look for others, as well. I grabbed a few and quickly put them on and removed them, not really caring because my dress was right there outside! And I needed to try it on! Impatiently, I wondered why they were taking so long to get it off the mannequin.

I began to glow when my skin first touched the satiny underlying layer of the dress. I officially felt like a bride.

"I love it," I told my mom and the consultant. "It's completely different from any other dress. It's exactly what I want."

With that settled, I moved onto other areas of planning. After the dress, the next most important item on my checklist was makeup. I have no problem admitting I'm a makeup junkie.

I had clear skin until I turned 21 and got mono. The viral infection, which I suspect was caused by drinking out of a deceivingly clean cup at a bookstore café I worked at for a total of two weeks, has since turned my life upside down. After being diagnosed with mono, I spent six months in bed watching *ALF* reruns on television. My liver and spleen were so enlarged that I was told I couldn't attend any concerts even if I had the energy to emerge from under my covers because if anyone accidently hit my stomach, the consequences would be severe. I have never felt 100 percent myself once I returned to the outside world, thanks to also being diagnosed with Epstein Barr virus and chronic fatigue syndrome, but I have certainly made damn well sure I look good!

I have always been adventurous with my makeup. One of my favorite looks around the time I first met Max was lining my top and bottom eyelids in florescent green shadow. It was a color only

I could wear. And as shocking as the style sounds, I actually received compliments!

The most memorable was from icons of modern day music, Thirty Seconds to Mars. I rocked that look when I went to the band's New York City hotel to interview them. While saying goodbye, I told them I would send a message when the issue was published. Tomo Miličević, the lead guitarist, told me to make sure I mentioned I was the girl with the bright green eye shadow. My look had obviously made an impression!

My bridal makeup had to be just as dramatic as my personal style and also have staying power to keep unflattering marks undercover. I scoured the Internet for makeup artists with a vision similar to my own. Many posts on my local New Jersey bridal forums raved about one woman in particular, Alexa Prisco, The Glam Fairy. Curious as to what the chatter was about, I crossed my fingers, searched Google and hoped that The Glam Fairy's work was as fabulous as her reputation.

Within seconds of landing on her official website, I knew I had struck glittery gold. Dramatic smoky eyes! Flawless airbrushed skin! Contoured cheekbones! Luscious lashes! We were definitely on the same sparkly page. I booked her services.

As a bride, I felt my most beautiful; from curled hair extensions to light pink painted toes. I was already counting down the weeks until I would be able to see the photo proofs.

The photographer for my wedding was a friend of mine from *Planet Verge*. I loved her journalistic style and trusted she would capture the vital details of the most important day of my life. Like, for instance, the petrified look on my new husband's face as we walked down the aisle after being pronounced husband and wife. Priceless.

We had a short, non-denominational ceremony in front of a charming gazebo. Due to partial paralysis caused by Multiple Sclerosis (MS), my father couldn't partake in the customary duty of walking me down the aisle. My mother was more than happy to lead the way.

At that moment, I realized I might be making a mistake by getting married. I didn't feel overwhelmed with emotion, like each step was bringing me closer to the father of my future children. I hoped everyone was wowed by my dress. I didn't wipe tears from my eyes as I read the vows I wrote for Max, I just prayed I could get through reading them in front of an audience and not mess up. Yet, I brushed it off and continued with the ceremony.

As I listened to Max read the vows I wrote for him, I realized why he might have had so much trouble writing his own in the first place. Maybe it wasn't because he didn't know how to put his love for me into words, but that he doubted our decision to marry, even though we had been living together for a year. Prefacing those vows I wrote for him, Max said, "It's kinda funny 'cause I always said I would never get married. People said I just hadn't met the right one, but when I met you I knew."

I know Max loved me, but I believe he was convincing himself to want the same things in life that I wanted. Perhaps he couldn't write his vows because he wasn't ready to give up his freedom, take responsibility for another person, and promise to one day be a good father to children he only told himself he wanted because I couldn't wait to be a mother.

My own vows began on an interesting note. I told Max, "I guess I should thank (my dog) Skye for turning you into a dog person, or we would not be here today." You'll notice I didn't begin with how much I loved him; I made reference to one of our struggles. When we first met, Max hated dogs and I actually stopped talking to him for a few months because I knew we could not have a future together. However, he eventually warmed up to Skye and her shedding fur.

Looking back, Max and I loved and needed each other in our lives for selfish reasons. But, as we made our relationship legal in front of all our family and friends, I realized it didn't matter if all the issues we had between us actually did change along with my last name. He wasn't my soul mate. I didn't feel emotional. I just knew that what I was experiencing was not what it was supposed to feel like when you marry the man of your dreams. He is not supposed to walk away from you after you walk down the aisle as husband and wife with tears in his eyes and tell you that he just needs to be alone because he is overwhelmed with emotion—love or anxiety, only he knows the truth. Nor is he supposed to leave your side during the entire reception. But that's what happened.

Max and I spent our wedding reception mingling with our own friends and family and only united to do the ceremonious cake cutting, stomach stuffing and garter toss. We didn't do the customary first dance because we both despised the act. I think it's awfully embarrassing and invasive for 150 of your closest friends and family to stand in a circle and watch you stupidly sway for three minutes. Half of them will cry because you're "so grown up" now, the other half because they feel lonely and are hoping they will have a chance to one day be on that dance floor. No, thank you.

I have always hated attending weddings and feel equally uncomfortable at events where I'm the center of attention. I didn't even attend my college graduation for fear of having to walk onto a stage in front of an audience to receive my diploma.

Yet, I became obsessed with planning the most creative, attention-to-detail wedding anyone would have ever attended. It came to the point that I was more focused on the wedding than the actual marriage. I started to brush off all the relationship problems that arose and hoped everything would settle into place after the wedding.

I put my entire heart and soul into planning even the most miniscule of details. There could not be anything generic. The most personal touch was a four-page magazine program all about Max and me, which included photos from our engagement shoot and a collage of memories through the years. It was such a hit, that I made another eight-page magazine called *The Newlyweds*, which included photos from the wedding, and sent to each guest as a thank-you.

Magazine creation was a huge part of my life, so it was only natural to include it in my big day. The same goes for music. Having spent years working in the music business, I formed friendships with some talented folks and of course had to incorporate them into the day's events as ceremony and reception musicians.

I also designed the seating cards and incorporated my precious fur-children, Skye (a Siberian husky/ German shepherd mix) and Lucky (a Korean jindo) into the day by using their pictures for the table assignments. Each table was named after a latte flavor.

A cupcake connoisseur, I was determined to incorporate the treats and used them as centerpieces. This was actually my friend Penny's idea. She and I were engaged at the same time, so we helped each other plan our weddings. She was one of three pin-up usherettes at my wedding.

We asked guests to sign a black acoustic guitar using hot pink and silver markers. I planned on using the guitar to decorate our newlywed home. (I should mention that I waited a year for Max to hang the guitar, but it remained in a corner of our living room for the duration of our marriage).

At the end of the night, the videographer pulled Max and me aside and asked us to say a message to our future selves. It was so awkward because we were both caught off guard and words did not naturally come to mind. The videographer must have seen the red flags waving high. However, it wouldn't be until after our honeymoon that those red flags would begin to flap in my face.

Two

My So-Called Marriage

After our wedding, Max and I flew to Antigua. But first, we had a layover in Puerto Rico. It was there that the first argument of our marriage took place.

Walking down the streets in the center of San Juan, we passed a man offering tourists photos with a beautiful parrot. Being a huge animal lover, I of course wanted to pose with the bird. However, the man selling the photos was very sketchy. Max didn't want me to participate, so he walked away, leaving me in a potentially dangerous situation. I was infuriated. I felt that a protective husband would've dragged his new wife down the sidewalk.

In addition to the parrot incident, the local cuisine was far from vegetarian friendly. I found it very hard to enjoy myself while my stomach was growling and I was fuming at my husband. However, I refused to let that ruin my time and focused my thoughts on Antigua, where our real honeymoon would begin.

The island was pure paradise. I even broke my anti-sunbathing rule and soaked up the sun's glow (with SPF 50). Aside from dodging jellyfish, it was delightfully refreshing to wade in the crystal clear water. And leave it to me to make friends with the stray dogs on the beach. It broke my heart to see so many homeless animals on the island and learn the locals considered them pests. I made sure they felt loved, snuck them food and swam with a pack of four.

Unfortunately, the honeymoon literally ended as soon as we returned home. They say the first year of marriage is the hardest. I never made it to the second year, so I can't tell you if it gets easier or not once you pass the 365-day mark. But I can tell you that during that one year I spent as a wife, I lost myself. I had always been optimistic and romantic. Marriage turned me into a sad, lonely woman who constantly fought with her husband about lack of intimacy.

Max wouldn't hold my hand in public, eat dinner with me, cuddle on our couch or go to bed the same time I fell asleep. He became my roommate and a very unattractive one at that. I refused to kiss him when he grew a beard, so of course he gave up shaving. It was his way of pulling away because he was unhappy being married, I believe.

There were a few factors that contributed to the death of my so-called marriage. For one thing, there was financial strain. I had a low-income music industry job and Max was frequently unemployed. He was still figuring out his passions and changed jobs a lot, sometimes without consulting me first. He wasn't happy with himself and I was frustrated with him. I needed him to get a job that provided health benefits so I could leave my job, which I felt was holding me back from furthering my dreams. We used my paychecks to cover the mortgage and lived off my credit cards, which piled up my debt. I resented Max because I not only worked full-time, but also spent my spare time trying to launch companies and take on freelance work to make extra money.

These issues could have been resolved over time. But one deal-breaker could not: children. The day Max told me he didn't want to be married anymore and that he never wanted to have children, even though he previously agreed to, it was over for me. I had been putting pressure on us to prepare for having a family. I wanted to be pregnant by age 30 and kept reminding Max that we needed to get our lives in order. I learned I should not have married a man who agreed to have kids with me. I needed a partner who could not wait to be a father. But I'll get to that part of my story later.

First, I want to tell you about the one week during the entire fourteen months of our marriage that Max and I were actually happy.

It was the week of our one-year anniversary. I remember being so blissful that we even ordered a miniature version of our wedding cake so we could eat it fresh, rather than the one-year-old frozen top that is customary.

I believed Max and I were going to make it after all and wanted to commemorate our renewed love. Well, nothing says forever like a tattoo.

As a female with visible body art, I always considered it odd I ended up marrying a man who did not have a dab of ink on his body. Max wasn't against tattoos, he just couldn't think of anything he wanted permanently etched. I wanted to initiate Max into tattooed society and our first wedding anniversary was the perfect occasion. I suggested we get matching "XO" tattoos on our wrists to represent our love and because we survived the bad times.

It's important to note that about six months into our marriage, Max and I actually made the decision to separate. Though it lasted about two weeks and we still lived together, I removed my wedding ring. This was in April, my birthday month. At this time, my music 'zine, *Planet Verge*, had transitioned into an Internet TV show and we hosted a launch party in New York City.

That night was one of the best of my musical life. Along with running *Planet Verge*, I had previously launched a music PR firm, Audio Crush, and recently scored the Matches, a wildly successful indie band, as clients. (Interesting tidbit, the Matches' vocalist Shawn Harris, an outspoken vegan, is the person who inspired me to give up eating chicken and become pescatarian. I interviewed

Shawn regarding veganism for one of the very first episodes of *Planet Verge* TV. Sadly, that part of the footage became lost so I never got to watch or release the interview.)

The Matches were showcasing in New York City from their hometown of Oakland, California, at my show! It was magical being surrounded by bands I loved and my best girls, the *Planet Verge* staff. It didn't matter that Max wasn't there. He just would've dragged me down. Every time I looked at my naked left ring finger, I felt free.

Yet, a few weeks later I slipped those diamonds back on my finger. Max and I had decided to try to work through our struggles. And I believed we had. So by the time our one-year anniversary rolled along, I figured we were in the clear to mark ourselves with each other's memory for life. Everything seemed to have fallen into place by that September.

Max liked the matching "XO" tattoo idea and even suggested we get them on opposite wrists for when we held hands. Yes, you read that correctly. I said when we held hands. Like two people who voluntarily touched each other in public. Shocking, but we were actually in love during that one week.

When we got to the tattoo parlor, the artist drew a few different options for the "XO" but recommended we make it even more personal by drawing our own. Max and I both decided that his handwriting was cooler than mine, so we chose his "XO." I had an inkling that getting matching tattoos would jinx our marriage, but pushed aside my signature paranoia. However, my instincts were in tune. Two months later, I moved out.

Now, I must state that I am not a quitter and leaving was far from the easy way out of my marriage. I did everything I could to make things work. I even begged Max to go to therapy. I pledged to be by his side for better or worse and richer or poorer, and I meant every word.

Like I mentioned earlier, I put pressure on us to build a nest egg, buy a house and have babies. On our track, I didn't see those milestones coming to fruition. I'm the most goal-oriented person

I know. Yet, somehow I ended up with someone who was still figuring out what he wanted in life. Regardless, I was dedicated to making our marriage work. I told him this shortly after our one-year anniversary. We were at our lowest point, basically leading two separate lives. Max frequently went out with his friend, Sam. It upset him that I didn't have the energy to be social on work nights, between battling chronic fatigue and running *Planet Verge* after-hours. Towards the end, he went out multiple times a week. We barely spent time together.

I was alone whether or not Max was home, so it really didn't make a difference. We were both miserable. I knew we didn't have the connection married couples were supposed to embody. Max realized this, as well.

It was his cousin Carey's wedding that made us face the truth. Carey was our age and she and I had become close during her wedding planning process, as I designed her magazine programs. At Carey's reception, a member of the bridal party gave a speech about how Carey and her husband were perfect for each other and even finished each other's sentences.

Max and I didn't finish each other's sentences. I didn't have any idea what was going through his mind. Hearing that speech assured me: I married the wrong man. The speech had the same effect on Max, but he actually had the guts to approach the subject. Deep down, we both knew we weren't compatible for the long haul.

One day, Max opened the floodgates to his feelings. Words spit like daggers from his mouth and stabbed my heart as he told me, "I don't want to be married. I don't know if I don't want to be married to anyone, or just you."

My body went into bloody shock. Fine, he didn't want to be married. But specifically not to me?! What was that supposed to mean? I was a great wife! Any man would be lucky to have me, that is, as long as he didn't mind cooking dinner every night.

I still hung onto a morsel of hope after Max's statement, knowing that sometimes you just need to talk about bottled up issues.

But what Max said next made me numb. He told me he never wanted to have children. This was my deal-breaker. Nothing else was worth working on if he could never give me the thing I wanted most in the world: motherhood.

My motherly/nesting instincts began at an early age. I used to catch inchworms and butterflies and make them homes in shoeboxes. I actually molded tissues into furniture!

What can I say? My mom raised me as a total girly-girl. I had every doll on the market—from those with battery-operated heartbeats to newborn baby dolls with lifelike gender parts. I even owned a pregnant doll. She had a swollen stomach that when removed, revealed a newborn inside. After the baby (mine was a girl!) was "born," a flat stomach popped up and just like magic, she was back to her amazing pre-maternity body. If only this happened in the real world, right?

I have always envied adorable pregnant people. So you can imagine how my world sank into the solar system when Max told me he never wanted children. That settled matters. It was over. I phoned a friend in the middle of night for solace and then cried myself to sleep.

The following morning, I called my mother in hysterics while I walked the dogs to tell her I was moving back home. This was not surprising news to her. She told me not to be sad, but happy that I could move on and get what I deserved.

When my father heard the news, he told me to freeze my eggs and file for divorce. If I had the money, I probably would have frozen my eggs. I was having a nervous breakdown because I was 28 years old and starting my life over from scratch.

Since I wanted to be pregnant by age 30, I put the pressure on Max. I told him that we had two years to get our act together and save for a house because I didn't want to be an older mother and everyone knows there are risks to having a baby after age 35. Our financial status had already led us to put our condo on the market. In an attempt to save money and reduce expenses, we planned on renting a place. I hoped with less financial stress, we would be able to get our relationship on track, enjoy each other's company and build our family.

It's my own fault for thinking I could change Max's view on fatherhood. But for a while, did think so. Very early in our relationship, I presented Max with an ultimatum. We were actually driving at the time. "If you never want children, I will get out of this car right now," I told him.

There was no way I was going to waste my time and invest feelings in someone who didn't want to have children. I felt too old to be casually dating.

Max knew if our relationship ended, I would cut him out of my life. He didn't want to lose me, so I believe he tried to convince himself that one day he would want his own rug rats. He lied to me and perhaps himself.

We even discussed names for boy and girl babies, some of which Max suggested. I thought he was coming around to the idea of fatherhood. But those children would never exist because I entrusted my love and dreams to someone who deep down knew all along that he didn't want the same things in life as his wife.

The day after Max and I decided to divorce, I went to work (against my mother's advice). I cried a river before arriving and during my lunch break on phone calls with friends, but I made it through the day. I was determined to carry on as usual.

I spent Thanksgiving night and Black Friday of that year moving out of my precious condo. I had wanted to leave two weeks earlier, but I was struck with illness and unable to pack. Then, I had to wait for the new bed my father generously bought me to arrive before I could begin sleeping at my mom's. The holiday was the perfect time to begin carrying boxes out since Max was at his parents' house and I had the place to myself.

Max offered to let me stay at our condo so I didn't have to up-root my life. But there was no way in hell I was going to be stuck paying a mortgage I couldn't afford. If Max wanted to tear my life apart, then he could deal with the condo until it sold. Luckily, he didn't put up a fight.

Fortunately, our whole divorce process was very simple and civil. The bed and couch were already his, so they remained in the condo. Everything else I pretty much paid for on my credit cards (hello, post-marriage debt), so I took those items. I did, however, leave the TV stand, coffee table, pots, pans and blender. There's no denying I am an awful cook and Max would actually make use of them.

As much as I was relieved to be out of an unhappy marriage, I was devastated to be leaving my new home. Living in that condo was my first time out on my own, so to speak. When we first moved in, it was the condo of hopes and dreams. I felt liberated to finally have a place of my own and was so excited to decorate. Like our wedding, I put so much attention into every little detail— from coat hooks to placemats for the dog food bowls. But it never became "home" because there were never any warm, loving feelings between those walls. The couch represented sadness because every time we sat on it, he pushed me away. The dining table just stood as a reminder that we never ate our meals together. That's not the way I imagined my happily ever after playing out.

On my final trip, my mom and Joey helped me carry out the contents of my life. Taking one last look around the vacant rooms, I took a deep breath and closed the door on that chapter of my life.

Once again, music became the soundtrack to my world. I found peace in listening to a breakup song by my favorite musician, Butch Walker.

With those lyrics as solace, I carried hope for a bright tomorrow close to my heart and crammed as much furniture as possible into my childhood bedroom. Before I moved in with Max, he and I had painted my bedroom walls hot pink. Returning with my barely broken in black furniture was a nice contrast. Everything else was piled into the garage: wedding gifts that were never opened, the fine china, picture frames that displayed moments of a life that seemed to be surreal because it came and went so fast. Some of those boxes are still unopened.

I grew up there and had everything I owned with me, yet I didn't feel like I belonged at the house anymore. My mom had recently gotten a new puppy, Emme, and was worried that my two big dogs would cause problems. Granted, Skye had a history of ripping apart the couch and biting the windowsill every time another dog walked by outside. So I kept Skye and Lucky locked in my bedroom with me for the first week or so upon my return. Most of the time, they were the only company I wanted around me, anyway.

I spent a lot of time alone, hurt that I never even had a chance to settle into marriage and enjoy the experience. From day one, Max and I were hit with financial problems. That strain only exacerbated the little annoying issues we had with each other. We never had the opportunity to be happy because we were always stressed out and in survival mode. But even if money hadn't been an issue, our marriage still would have ended. I suppose I was grateful that we didn't prolong the inevitable and I got out while I was still young. But that didn't make my situation any better.

A few weeks after I settled in back at my mom's, I was let go from my job. The company for which I worked was struggling to keep afloat and my position was the first to be eliminated. Just my luck! When my boss broke the news, I was shocked. I was a hard worker, always developing innovative ideas to propel the company. I never imagined that would happen. But there I was, 28 years old, divorcing and jobless.

From that point on, I spent a lot of time sitting outside in the yard. The dogs chased each other in the sunshine while I collected my thoughts on paper.

Here are two experts from my diary:

March 6th (breakdown day)

"They're all assholes, Joelle. Just to different degrees."
-Mom

I cried a lot today. Max will only talk to me through text message. He said "I can't see you right now. I am where you were three or four months ago."

I just want to talk to him, see him, both agree that this is best for us. Not hate each other.

I am hurt that this happened. That he selfishly knew he didn't want to be married, but went through the motions. (Max actually spoke in person with my mom before I moved back home. He felt he owed her an explanation and told her that he had many conversations with his parents before our wedding about whether or not he was ready. Turns out he wasn't.)

I'm mad that I had a beautiful wedding and can never put up a picture of me as a bride. Or any nice family photos we took that day.

I just watched our wedding video. I see his clean shaven face—that's the man I love(d). Look how he voluntarily kissed me and put his arm around my waist. That never happened in real life.

Emme is barking right now. Almost as if to say "Joelle! Wake up! Stop remembering something good! The reality is that you were unhappy every day of that marriage. Sad. Alone. Depressed. That is what your life had become."

I'm remembering that one-week around our first wedding anniversary. We were honestly happy. I felt in love, leaving our condo and walking hand in hand to our car in the parking lot. We were happy. I was so happy. One week.

I have this matching "XO" tattoo in Max's handwriting on my wrist to commemorate it. Ick.

March 7th

I can't believe I didn't write in a diary for the past five years! Probably the most important in my life thus far—my whole relationship with Max. I don't want to ever forget it, as I mourn and move on. I'm a positive person. I know that everything happens for a reason. I don't regret our marriage. I wouldn't even have Lucky if I didn't get married. I'm sure at one point, I was happy. But I can't remember it. I don't know what happened, how we lost it, why we're both giving up. I have to walk away or I'll live my life in regret and unhappiness.

I'm sitting in the yard now. All three dogs are running around. It's muddy because the snow has melted. I'm wrapped in a hoodie and purple blanket. The birds are chirping and wind chimes are singing. All should be peaceful. But I'm burnt out. I couldn't fall asleep until 4 a.m. last night. Heart races. Nervous wreck.

As I mentioned in my diary, anxious thoughts drove my mind in a million different directions every night. In addition to the divorce and job loss, I felt like a loser moving back home. It was so embarrassing having to face all my brother's friends, especially on Saturday nights when I was home and they were all living it up in our basement.

My own social life had taken a turn as abruptly as my marriage. It's during times of crisis that you find who has your back. I parted ways with some of my best friends because I felt they did not understand or support what I was going through.

By the time I got my wedding album back from the photographer, almost all the key players from the ceremony were out of my life. Did I feel vacant? Certainly. But did I let that rule me? Not once.

Living in New Jersey, the state with the lowest number of divorces in the country, I was pretty sure I was the only woman divorced before age 30. After all, according to social media, everyone else my age was getting married and having babies. Meanwhile, I was a member of an underground society of women who had failed ourselves, our families, and our dreams of happily-ever-after. Or so it seems when it first happens.

When my marriage first ended, I couldn't relate to any books on the market. There were books from therapists filled with marriage-saving strategies and books with stories from mothers who spent decades as wives. I didn't want to save my marriage so that nixed the majority of books on the shelves. I did read one collection of divorce stories, but found it hard to relate to women who had children my age.

I knew there were other women out there just like me, who felt so alone, like they were the only ones going through divorce in their 20s. I just had to find them. One night right after I left Max, Penny and I went to dinner to celebrate our 10-year "friendiversary." Walking back to our cars in the parking lot, I told her, "One day, I'm going to write a book about this."

I felt it was important to unite with young, confident divorced women so we could lead the way for those whose lives were just turning down this winding road. I wanted to show new twenty-something divorcées that the end of marriage is just the beginning of the lives we were meant to live. And that life is indeed beautiful.

From that point on, I embraced the opportunity to select the people who I felt deserved my friendship, love and talents. But before I could officially celebrate divorce in my 20s, I had to forgive myself for marrying Max and take creative measures to release anger. So, I made a "Good Riddance" list of everything I disliked about Max, compiled a list of everything I sought in a future mate and trashed my wedding dress.

These liberating rituals allowed me to celebrate my divorce. I'll tell you about them and then I'll share what I've learned from young, confident and successful divorced women around the world.

Three

Write a "Good Riddance" List

There are two essential items every newly divorced woman must have within reach at all times: a pen and a notebook.

There are going to be times, especially in the beginning of the divorce process, when nostalgia hits, tears fall and we find ourselves mourning. That's when we need to read our "Good Riddance" lists. Nothing is a better snap back to reality than reliving all the moments that led up to D-day.

It's important that as divorced women, we always remember that our marriages ended for a reason. If our marriages were just based on the moments that made us smile, then they would still exist. The reality is that those memories were likely few and far between. The large gaps are filled with disappointing events, annoying habits, lonely nights and irresolvable issues.

Because I regrettably didn't maintain a diary during my entire relationship with Max, when we first split up, I decided to make a "Good Riddance" list. I wanted to make sure I would always be able to remember why it ended and could never look back and doubt my decision.

Every time I thought of something negative about Max, I jotted it down. This process was a huge release of pent up anger. Every drip of ink from my pen sent my feelings to the wind. Today, an arsenal of "Good Riddance" pages later, I no longer blame myself for getting married and divorced. Instead, I'm proud I took a risk and removed myself from the situation.

Now, whenever any of my friends are going through a break-up, I recommend they make a "Good Riddance" list, too. My advice actually made it into a song! My friend and former client Jean Paul Makhlouf from the band Cash Cash was particularly upset about the end of a long-term relationship. I suggested he make a list of all the negative things about his ex-girlfriend. He not only did that, he mentioned it in a song on his next album.

Of course we can't all record songs based on our "Good Riddance" lists, but we can still write off our ex-husbands!

My "Good Riddance" list consists of 63 items. At the top of that list is the day I found a stray dog with a big scar by his eye on the street during a thunderstorm and Max wouldn't come help me get him to our local animal shelter even though I pleaded and told him how important it was for me to help an animal. He didn't want me to get attached to the dog. It evoked the biggest fight in the history of our relationship. Even though he won the initial battle, I prevailed in the long run. Weeks later, finally with Max's approval, I ended up adopting the dog (Lucky) after no one claimed him at the shelter. Lucky has been my shadow since the day I brought him home, offers me unconditional love and puts a smile on my face every day.

There's one particular reason I considered adding to my "Good Riddance" list, but then decided against because I was actually grateful for the incident. It was the last time I saw Max before I moved out. With both of my dogs on leashes, I opened the door of the home I poured my heart and soul into building and told Max I didn't know if I'd be back that night. He didn't reply. He just let me go. As much as I knew I had to leave, I wanted him to plead with me to stay and tell me things didn't have to end, that we could find a way to mend our marriage. I was scared to start over and leave a life in which I was comfortable, even though I was miserable.

While it hurt because Max didn't put up a fight, it was the best course of action. I acknowledged that he really never completely had my heart. Rather, I loved him like a best friend, an essential person but not my life partner. I'm not sure how he viewed me.

I took drastic measures when Max and I spilt up to reclaim my life, or at least my hair. I went to a cheap chain salon and instructed them to chop bangs. He had convinced me to grow mine out. The new look was exactly what I needed to say goodbye forever to Max. If we were to cross paths, he would know that he no longer owned my hair. It was liberating.

I'll admit that haircuts were the only time I slightly missed Max. Once, after we split, my professional-quality blow dryer broke and Max was nice enough to get me a replacement. However, I felt guilty calling upon him for my own selfish needs, so I adjusted to life as a regular hair consumer. All the discounted and top of the line beauty products in the world couldn't force me to stay in that unhappy marriage or continue an unhealthy friendship. I had to let go of everything to truly move on.

When I left Max and closed the door of the condo I called home for the final time, I knew I deserved better and made a vow to find my real soul mate. Naturally, I made a list to assist in my mission.

Four

Make a Dating Checklist

A ny newly divorced woman will tell you that re-entering the dating world is a frightening situation. Eventually, we have to face the scenario when we're first lured by a new man's bait. After we've been caught, we find ourselves gasping for air while he contemplates whether he would like to get cookin' or toss us back into the cold, crowded waters. He's playing the game, and we're so revitalized and ready to find a worthy love and get back to where we were in life that some of us are already envisioning walking down the aisle again.

It's natural to get overly excited. Most of us have been deprived of romance for so long, that we're eager to kick off our panties for passion. So we do. And then, the man who popped our post-divorce cherry won't reply to text messages for three days. Or, we'll see on his social media profile that all his new friends are hot women he seems to have met on a dating site.

When this happens, ladies, refer to your dating checklist. This document should compile all your requirements in a future mate.

Were you ignoring the fact that he lacked goals or disliked children because you drowned every time you looked into his oceanic eyes? If so, consider a dating checklist your lifeguard.

These bulleted items will not only help you find Mr. Right, but comfort you each time you encounter Mr. Eh, Mr. Playing-The-Field and Mr. I-Really-Thought-He-Was-The-One-This-Time-Even-Though-I-Only-Dated-Him-For-One-Week.

Divorce is a rejuvenating experience. It's a chance to explore interests and goals that have been simmering on the backburner of your brain. It's an arrow shot straight from cupid with a note attached that reads, "This is your second chance to get everything you want and deserve. Go for it."

Both your "Good Riddance" list and your dating checklist will be therapeutic and inspiring guides for this exciting new journey. Sometimes the "Good Riddance" list will act as your inner conscience and scream "Move on!"

One day, your dating checklist will have every quality marked off and you'll find yourself over the moon, not only with the person you've found, but also the person you have become. It happened to me.

My post-divorce dating checklist was rather simple. I wanted someone who:

- Was goal oriented
- Had a good job (or was taking action towards getting one)
- Was hard-working
- Had his own hobbies
- Appreciated all my hard work and supported my goals
- Loved my dogs
- Was open to fostering shelter dogs
- Embraced the straight-edge lifestyle or was close to it (Social drinking is OK. Getting drunk and using drugs are not. I've never smoked or had more than a sip of alcohol).
- Perhaps had tattoos

- Enjoyed the simple things in life
- I didn't have to chase or make all the first moves with
- Would happily take pictures with me (Max complained every time and even stomped off during our engagement photo shoot!)
- Enjoyed hanging out at book stores
- I didn't have to change who I was in order to be with
- Did not have stretched earlobes (Hey, it was a trend in my "scene!")
- Was not a musician (Touring all the time? Groupies? Always struggling financially? No, way!)

Eight months after I left Max, I met someone who met all my requirements! His name is Frank and at the time I write this chapter, I can state that we have been happily committed for over two years. I'll tell you more about Frank in a bit, though.

Right now, I want to share how I got back in the game. Judge me however you would like, but I went out on a date about a week or two after I left Max. Hey, it's not like I was mourning the end of a great romance! I was celebrating my rebirth. Yet, I let go of a few of my closest friends because they didn't approve of my decision to date so soon. Their loss, not mine! I can only have positive, supportive people in my life.

Anyway, I met up with a friend from college—let's call him Kyle—who had just gotten out of a long-term relationship, too. I had always crushed on Kyle, but unfortunately nothing ever progressed between us in college or that night. It was a bummer, but just not meant to be! However, it was nice to get dressed up and break into single life.

Since I've always been a bit of a homebody, I wasn't sure how to begin dating again. Luckily, I had a little help from friends, old and new. First, the *Planet Verge* girls came to my rescue. A few told me to sign up for a particular dating website, noting they met some decent guys. If nothing else, I was told the emails I received from site users would make me feel good about myself.

Within my first week on the site, I met Rick. It turned out we attended the same high school and had mutual friends. Having a connection between the virtual and real worlds made me feel a lot more comfortable about going on a date.

That night, Rick let me choose the restaurant, so I picked my favorite vegetarian establishment. Afterwards, we went back to his place. That resulted in my post-divorce one-night stand. Boy, did that make me feel alive! Of course, I didn't plan on our rendezvous to happen at all or for it to be a one-time deal, but it happened. And I don't regret going all the way. How could I resist such passion when it was lacking in my own life for so long?

I was crushed days later when I saw Rick tagged in online photos celebrating New Year's Eve with another woman while I was home alone with my dogs, hiding from society! My stomach sank every time I looked at their faces. Their tryst destroyed me for a few weeks. Vulnerable, I was convinced I was meant to meet Rick and my whole divorce happened so he could enter my life. If only I had my dating checklist together at that point! What was I thinking? He had a cat!

My spirits lifted when an old friend from high school, Molly, reached out to me. She saw my online status change from "married" to "divorced" and sent me a private message expressing her sympathy. We made plans to meet for brunch.

Over pancakes and coffee, Molly slowly approached the subject of our mutual online friend, Rick. She asked if he was the guy I was referring to having recently played me out. It turned out that Rick was Molly's ex–boyfriend! We bonded over our dating experiences. So, I have Rick to thank for not only making me feel like a sexual being again, but bringing a new confidant into my life.

Molly wasn't the only schoolmate who reached out to me during my dreaded status change. Another acquaintance of mine commented, "Sorry to hear, but believe me, life after divorce is so much better."

As horrible as it sounds, I was thrilled that this girl was divorced. I was no longer the lone wolf! I was slowly forming a pack!

We met for coffee, exchanged stories and laughed about our ex-husbands. She played an integral role in helping me deal with my divorce. Sure, friends and family help, but only another young divorced woman can relate to all the emotions we're feeling as we navigate the post-divorce world.

This friend was also dating online. We helped each other write bios and choose photos for our profiles. Whenever we went on a date, we made sure to take all precautions. I'll discuss online dating more in-depth later, but basically, we would investigate other dating sites to see if the guy kept multiple profiles. Then, we checked social media sites to make sure he was "normal." Once a date was set, we e-mailed each other all the details of where we were meeting (always a public place) and the guy's vital information including phone number, full name, email and home address.

I only met two other guys from a dating site. The first was a heavily tattooed hipster who worked on Wall Street and had just broken up with his girlfriend. We talked for months before I went into New York City to meet Mr. Hipster at his job and then accompany him to a going away party for his friend. He was adorable, but younger and very shy. I don't think he was ready for another relationship. The poor dude was really heartbroken. That was fine with me because he liked girls who wore glasses and minimal makeup. On dates, I wear contacts and Urban Decay glitter-specked eye shadow. Next!

When May rolled around, six months after Max and I split, I decided to pay a visit to Ajnira, a spiritual healer. Below is the transcript from my tarot card reading. Please note, Ajnira did not receive any prior insight on my situation, yet nailed my relationship with Max.

"You're freaking out," Ajnira told me. "There's a lot of things that are happening to you—ideas and thoughts from all directions."

She continued, "You have a problem with someone. They've been thinking a lot about you. You're estranged from this person. There's been a rift—even though you're actually still in contact, you're separated, alienated. It feels as though you're living in separate worlds."

Ajnira seemed to be reading my mind when she said, "You've been standing on this conviction that you are right and no matter which way you cut it, you are right. There's no disputing. You're not apologizing and there's no going back. There's nothing to rehash, your mind is completely made up. It's so completely made up that as far as you're concerned, it's over. It's in the past, it doesn't exist for you anymore; you cut them loose and you cut this whole situation out of your life."

Wowed, I listened intently as Ajnira elaborated, "You are trying to bring yourself together with all the things that you want to be involved with. The things you want to be involved with are things that provide you the opportunity for long-term security: financial, emotional and practical. There was a deal-breaker situation. That's what we make changes for. That's why there are situations that evolve that show us someone's true colors. It's good to see when a situation shows you how much time you're wasting and how little common ground you thought you had and also that your expectations and their expectations and beliefs are completely different."

At that point, I informed Ajnria of my pending divorce. She then continued her reading.

"In your very near future, it looks as though you're going to be overwhelmed with a passionate situation," Ajnira said next. "You're going to be very highly involved—sexually, passionately involved—with somebody. You're going to be focusing on that. You have the time and focus now to participate in that more. That brings you a lot of happiness; it's a good situation. You're finding your feet on the ground again, where you can actually move forward and you can feel the feelings that you should've been feeling all along in your marriage, but it took this to wake you up to let you know that what you were getting in your marriage wasn't the way it really was supposed to be."

"Whoo! Finally," I thought to myself.

The reading continued. "Now, all this energy that you have should be focused on things that matter to you—things that have heartfelt significance, things that you care about, and only those things. Wherever you put your energy, it drains your life force if it's not fulfilling or if it's not returning to you equal and appropriate energy in exchange. So your spiritual guides are basically saying you're doing the right thing because you're not wasting any more time, you're not going down any more roads that are bringing you nowhere and that the things you focus on expand."

After taking a moment to mentally thank my spiritual guides, I turned back to Ajnira. "The fabric of reality is very fragile. Every minute it could just dissolve and your life could fall apart or it could come together in amazing ways. Despite appearances, the things that you've asked for are in the process of being achieved. Very shortly, you'll be standing on top of the world because you made certain goals your object and they are being achieved. Then, you'll have to make new goals."

Once again, Ajnira was dead on when she noted, "It does seem that your husband doesn't really believe in the divorce. Is that true?"

That was indeed true! I recently ran into Max at a concert. He got so upset upon seeing me that he relocated to a different section. Later that night, he called and tearfully said he thought we would still go out on dates after our split! He wondered what would happen if we worked things out. I told him that I never planned on seeing him again. He respected my honesty and remorsefully told me that if he knew what he wanted in life, this never would've happened. I replied to him, "If you knew what you wanted in life, this never would have happened because it's the opposite of what I want."

But, back to Ajnira, who told me, "I think he is hoping that it will somehow be reconciled and you'll come back together again and you'll realize the reasons why you married him in the first place. He's still very much in love with you. Oh well! You tried it."

Those were my thoughts exactly. "It didn't work for you," confirmed Ajnira. "You're taking your magic tools—you're a magician in your own life, creating your reality. You are able to create anything you want because you're a highly developed, evolved person and you know how things work for you. At least you're not confused, because a lot of people would stay in a situation, trying to work it out and see things from the other person's point of view. You're honoring yourself and that takes a lot of courage and self-confidence."

Pegging my personality, Ajnira then said, "But you do worry about other things and go into states of being immersed in your own world and you don't notice what's going on outside your life because you're so self-absorbed in your interior world. You have a lot of blessings that are being offered to you that you may not even be aware of because you're so caught up in this self-contained situation. Your spiritual guides are just saying, whenever there's any kind of difficulty in your life—like losing your job, let's say—it's supposed to bring you to this place where you stay objective, where you don't let it rock you, where nothing happens to your stability (mentally and emotionally) where you just seek to iron out whatever issues keep surfacing and repeating. If this situation mirrors in any way a prior pattern that you have that's not serving you, the sooner you get the message and the lesson, then it can collect and be over."

What Ajnira said next helped me understand why I was meant to lose my job. "You're now in this phase where you want to cut and make something happen that's new and so it kinda leaked over into your job, too. You just got sick and tired of everything you were doing and wanted to turn over a new leaf. This is all about you testing yourself to see if you can be thrown into situations that are outside your comfort zone, situations that you can't predict and that you're not well-versed in, so you can raise the bar in your personal ability to adapt and to create something new."

My heart sped up a bit as Anjira told me, "You're going down the path of your life and you have everything that you need to navigate the road in front of you. Life is uncertain. The more, in a sense, you get used to dealing with uncertainty, and feel that you have the inner resources to handle whatever comes, the more prepared you will be when things happen that you don't anticipate. There is a job that you'll be getting, and you'll be getting a phone call about, but you haven't applied yet."

On a side note, it turned out Ajnira was right. I turned down the first job I was offered, but five months later accepted a position at a public relations firm.

Back to the reading. Ajnira explained, "There are certain issues that keep coming up for you and will be reflected in both places. Whatever's coming up in your personal life will come up in your business life. There's this bleed-through effect. You want to be in a really good connected relationship where you're choosing to have it all and you're being guided. You have a lot of spiritual leaders walking with you, whispering in your ear, taking every step with you. You're being protected and it looks like everything you ask for at this point in your life, you actually get. You just have to be sure to be clear and actually express it. Just put it out there and the things that can meet it will meet you."

Nearing the end of the reading, Ajnira said, "You're putting down a new foundation in your life with the standards and boundaries that you want to operate and as you do this, everyone you meet and come in contact with applies. The secret to the success that you're having is a place of detachment. Buddha says that the cause of all suffering is attachment and the path of freedom is detachment. By you dancing over the surface of your life as if you do not have any problems at all, even though there are problems, that minimizes the problem. That brings you to this place where the problems are also the source of our great benefits, our great wealth."

"The world is a mirror of what goes on inside of us internally," Ajnira informed me. "So when we see what's being reflected at us, we know where we're at and that's 100 percent confirmation of what we're vibrating in terms of a frequency and the law of attraction—how we're vibrating. Since you don't have any white-knuckle clenching emotion, the things that you're asking for can come to you. Even though they're not immediate, they're in the works. They just need an accumulation of energy to be present in your 'now.' All of this is about you wiping the slate clean and making a new beginning. It's more exciting actually, if a little treacherous, because you're on your toes. You're really like the heroine in the novel of the adventure of your life."

Ajnira assured me, "There are no wrong moves; there's just finding the formula of how you run your life and sticking to it."

I encourage all young divorcées to note what Ajnira told me next: "By taking back your freedom from this whole commitment of marriage, you're becoming the sovereign ruler of your world. You're getting your ticket back. You can create all rules for how everyone interacts with you and the rules that you live by and it's just something that you won't be giving up again. So even though you want to be in a deeply committed, connected, passionate, intimate relationship, you won't be giving up control. You won't be giving up your independence."

Ajnira concluded my reading saying, "There are just things you've learned from the whole experience of marriage. Marriage is difficult. It's not a walk in the park. It's not the fantasy of it that we're always told when we're little, this whole big fairytale. We give up a piece of ourselves in order to be involved in that way. When we need ourselves back, which we ultimately do, we have to carve it out of that unit. So now, you'll be protecting yourself instead of being in a situation feeling that you have to sacrifice yourself for the benefit of the relationship."

Meeting with Ajnira put me at ease. I felt hopeful and calm. One month after my tarot reading with Ajnira, I met the man who would become my boyfriend, Frank. They say love finds you when you least expect it and I certainly didn't plan on meeting my soul mate in a dirty rock 'n' roll bar called the Court Tavern. In fact, I wasn't on the prowl at all that night.

I was a few weeks into hanging out with this guy I had met online. Turns out we once again had mutual friends. He was a little dorky but rode a motorcycle. He also owned a house. However, smart financial decisions were not enough to keep me playing along with his text message games. I found them to be emotionally draining!

This guy sometimes waited hours or days to reply to texts and on top of that, never took me on a proper date. We always hung out with his friends. There were also a few evident deal-breakers on my dating checklist, like his occasional smoking. I knew I would have to eventually spread my wings and fly away, but wanted to wait until he returned from a business trip to confirm that it was over. This may sound odd, but I felt like a player talking to more than one guy, although I know that is what dating is all about. What can I say? I'm a monogamist!

With that said, I obviously didn't feel right talking to anyone else until I made it clear to motorcycle man that I was no longer interested in playing games. Still "involved," I wasn't expecting to be talking to guys the night I met Frank. Besides, I was technically working.

My friends Nicole, Jessica and I were filming an episode of *Planet Verge* TV with a band we knew. The guitar player had one of his good friends, Frank, with him that night. Frank's not a musician, which would've crossed him off my list, but he did go on tour with the band sometimes. We met up with everyone before the show.

That night, I held the role of videographer while Nicole interviewed the group. Frank watched and then we all went our separate ways for dinner.

Later at the show, the *Planet Verge* girls and I went to relax in the back room of the venue so we could chat and avoid the noise of the opening acts. Shortly after, Frank and his friend joined our coffee klatch. Frank had me laughing all evening. It wasn't long before I said to myself, "I could date him."

This may sound funny, but the first thing that attracted me to Frank was his voice. I just love it. Frank also shaves his head, just like my teenage crush, surfer Kelly Slater. Frank may not be a world-champion surfer, but he was captain of the swim team and a lifeguard (Hobbies? Check!) I look up to him—literally. At 6'3", Frank towers over my 5'1" frame. Because of that, I always feel protected when I'm in his arms, which have a few tattoos. He doesn't have as many or as large tattoos as I do, however. In fact, Frank doesn't really like girls with tattoos. He especially isn't fond of the huge calligraphic "sXe" tattoo on my forearm that I got on my 25th birthday to represent being straight-edge.

However, I can't blame him. That tattoo was supposed to be really small and on my wrist. But when the artist showed me his sketch, I loved it so much that I went ahead with the recommended size and placement. Then, I went home and cried, afraid to remove the bandage from my arm. Once I did, I hid it from my mother for weeks. I woke up every day looking at my arm, hoping it was just a bad dream. Today, it's my favorite tattoo. I love that no matter what I wear, my skin shows the world I am artistic and strong. The only annoying thing about my body art is covering it up for my corporate job, which I never thought I would have!

Luckily, Frank saw beyond my tattoos and fell in love with my total package. Ok, mostly my booty, as he likes to say. But there was really no talk of tattoos the night we met.

Rather, our little group tested each other on *Saved by the Bell* trivia, which Frank totally won. At one point, I told him I am obsessed with soap operas.

"You're like a 49-year-old divorced lady," he teased.

I figured that was as good a time as any to come clean. "Actually, a 29-year-old divorced lady!," I retorted.

It was always so awkward having to reveal that part of my past to guys I just met. I could just imagine their brains going crazy trying to figure out my deep, dark secrets. Being divorced can sometimes feel like there is a great big red stamp on your forehead that says "baggage."

Our conversation continued, but eventually our circle parted ways as the band set up their instruments to perform. Frank didn't speak to me the rest of the night. I was convinced it was because he didn't want to date a girl with a gritty past. But a few days later, he sent me a friend request online and invited me for a "non-threatening" cup of coffee, which I thought was adorable and clever. I accepted his offer but delayed setting an actual date.

At the time, I was trying to balance my unemployment by taking on babysitting jobs, working very briefly as a part-time bridal consultant (oh, the irony) and doing casting for a reality TV show. Babysitting may sound like an odd job for a 29-year-old, but I loved it. I began filling in for my friend Megan on her nanny gigs and then got hired by a friend of one of the families.

My charge was the most adorable five-year-old ever, who was coincidently named Noelle. She had platinum blonde hair, piercing blue eyes and a toy husky. It was meant to be. Babysitting Noelle was more than just a job. It allowed me to play house and pretend to be a mom for a few hours every week. However, I felt that void in my life more than ever during those nights.

Between scouting television talent, convincing a five-year-old to go to bed at her scheduled time, and sending out resumes, my days were long and draining. In addition, part of me was reluctant.

As much as I wanted to be in a new, healthy relationship, I was afraid I would lose all the freedom I had just regained. I was taking online classes through unemployment to get certified in two programs I hoped would assist me in getting a graphic design job at a magazine.

In addition, a friend was teaching me professional video editing. That program advanced my skills for *Planet Verge* TV. I hoped to finally get *Planet Verge* to the big time! We had just launched a few documentary series and I felt like my life was finally picking up speed. For the first time, I had the freedom to chase all my career-related dreams and hours to dedicate towards growing projects. The workaholic in me feared distraction.

But then, I realized Frank was the only person whose phone calls I accepted during *General Hospital*. And I found myself constantly checking my phone to see if he sent me a text, which he did at least once every three hours. I wanted to talk to Frank and hear about his days.

I learned that Frank and I had a lot in common. He likes basically the same music as I do, hates drug use, rescued a shelter dog, and has strong family values. Check! Check! Check! Check!

Frank made it very clear that he was interested in becoming more than friends. Check "Someone I didn't have to chase or make all the first moves with" off my list! Frank sent me "good morning" text messages, affectionately nicknamed me Jasper (Joelle + Casper because I'm so pale), and always put a smile on my face.

On our first real date, we sat on a park bench and ate ice cream (Enjoys the simple things in life—Check!). Then, we walked around the artsy little town. As we passed a sushi restaurant and perused the menu, Frank said, "We'll eat here one night."

I knew right then and there that Frank wasn't the type of guy to play games. He was genuine and our chemistry was organic. Everything felt natural. Without even thinking about it, I missed *General Hospital* on SoapNet (RIP, network) that night.

The next time Frank and I hung out, we went shopping so he could pick up supplies for an upcoming camping trip. Any other girl would've scoffed at that date, but I'm not high maintenance. Afterwards, we stopped by his apartment.

I know where your mind is going, so let me stop you before it gets to the bedroom! Frank took me to meet his dog, Linus, the beagle he rescued from a shelter with his roommate.

I was impressed by all the tricks Frank taught Linus. The dog could even play hide and seek! I made a mental note to have Frank train my wild pack. The rest of the night was spent sitting on the couch watching television, Frank with his arm around me and Linus cuddling across our laps. I felt like we were a little family already.

The next week, Frank volunteered to come over and bathe Skye and Lucky. I was bit nervous because he would be the first guy I brought home post-divorce. But I worried for no reason.

While at my house, Frank struck up conversation with my mom and then entered the warzone. See, I tried to tell him that bathing my dogs was no easy feat. Being the stubborn Taurus (I am one year and four days older) that he is, Frank refused to listen. However, he learned his lesson as Skye and Lucky turned into bucking broncos and had to be muzzled. From that day on, Frank made it his mission to train the dogs, which I've found super attractive.

A few months following that afternoon, I changed my online status; this time, to "in a relationship" with Frank.

It was wild falling in love while still legally married. Frank joked that he was having an affair with a married woman. But on September 9th—just 12 days before what would have been my second wedding anniversary—I sent Frank a humorous text message from the courthouse that said "Dear Frank, our love affair can now go public and we can consummate our relationship." My divorce was official.

Fortunately, my whole divorce filing process was very simple. My mother, a legal secretary, took pride in typing up the paper work. The day of proceedings, my mom, lawyer and I sat in a room full of people who were also scheduled to go before the judge for their divorces. I was the youngest person there and felt so out of place. Max didn't contest the divorce, so he didn't attend. I notified him by text message to expect the paperwork and all he had to do was sign on the dotted line.

When the judge called my name, I approached the bench and confirmed some information, like the address of my marital residence, before he declared me a free woman. Of course, I considered myself free since the day I left Max, but it was nice to make things legal.

My divorce day was far from bittersweet. By that point, I was already in love with Frank and bursting at the seams to confess my feelings. In just a few months, Frank showed me love and what it was like to be in a real relationship.

I've loved before, but have come to realize I romanticized my previous relationships. Before I met Frank I always considered Brad, my on-again-off-again boyfriend of four years during college, to be my greatest love. From kisses to love notes hidden under pillows, Brad introduced me to fairy tale romance.

However, he often chose partying with his friends over me, his girlfriend. We were both workaholics so I thought it was OK that he chose HTML codes for clients over cuddles. Also, his friends didn't like me because I didn't drink, so sometimes Brad let an entire month go by without seeing me. I didn't know any better at the time to realize it was not a healthy relationship. We spent holidays together, and Brad often wrote me songs, poems and gushy emails, so I overlooked my place on his list of priorities.

When I first met Max, I didn't think another love could compare to the way I felt about Brad. So I stopped looking for that intense spark and enjoyed the comfortable nature of my relationship with Max. He didn't shower me with affection, but Max was there when I needed emotional support. Our similar interests drew us to each other, but couldn't be the glue that bonded our delicate relationship.

Today, I don't have to worry about anything coming between Frank and I. From the names of our children to the breeds of dogs we're going to adopt, the future Frank and I will share is just waiting for us to catch up. Every day, we're a little closer to our goals. One of which is moving into our own place.

For a while, Frank was living about an hour away from me, which began to take its toll. Because I was financially devastated from the loss of my job and buried in credit card debt from paying off my past (wedding expenses, honeymoon, condo), I was in no position to move out of my mom's house in order to get a place with Frank. Plus, my brother was no longer living at home, so there was plenty of room. In no rush to leave, I asked Frank to move in and have been falling asleep with my head on his chest ever since.

Sharing space with Frank meant sharing closets. Every morning as Frank slid the closet doors open to get dressed, he was blinded by a bright, sparkling obstruction: my wedding gown. I knew I had to get rid of it, and since I needed the extra cash, I figured my best option was to put it up for sale. I listed my dress on websites and even consulted with a bridal consignment shop but was left frustrated by the lack of money I would actually make, when or *if* it sold.

I was stuck with a work of art I never wanted to view again. My wedding dress became a constant reminder of my failed marriage. Every time I looked at it, I became angry thinking of how beautiful I looked the day I wore it and got upset because I couldn't hang up any pictures of myself wearing it.

Then it hit me. I didn't need to sell my dress to get rid of it. I could trash it during a glamorous photo shoot.

Five

Cut Away the Past

I cut up my wedding dress. The $1,600 exquisite ivory, intricately beaded, floral, drop-waist, sweetheart neckline, designer gown that I wore on what was supposed to be the happiest day of my life; the day that I planned on as being my gateway to happily ever after. I sliced into it with scissors and ripped it apart with my bare hands, performing my own open-heart surgery—on national television.

After my wedding, I stayed in touch with Alexa, my makeup artist. When *Planet Verge* launched our Internet TV show, Alexa offered to do the makeup for our host photo shoot. I had been married for about six months at that time and as you know, Max and I were already on the rocks, which I confided to Alexa. Not long after that day, Alexa was cast on a popular reality television show, which led to her own spin-off.

By the time her spin-off entered production, I was divorced and a few months into working on my new project, this book! I enlisted Alexa to do my makeup for my "trash the dress" photo shoot. It ended up airing on an episode of her show and the producers even threw in a hair makeover for me.

You will recall that the only thing I missed about Max was his talent for cutting my hair. Finding a stylist to replace him had been a series of disastrous adventures and I hoped this makeover would give me my edge back. I anticipated looking in the mirror afterwards and feeling like my old self.

That didn't quite happen. As viewers across the country witnessed, I was mortified when I first looked in the mirror after my hair makeover. The short pixie crop showed my ears. If there is one thing I dislike about myself, it's my big ears. Not only was the cut way shorter than I expected, but I wasn't a fan of the black and red color blocking technique at first. Everyone else raved over it. Maybe I did look out-of-this-world, as in out of a world in which I would ever live!

Nevertheless, I dug up my confidence and forged ahead with the photo shoot. Once my makeup was on, I actually felt pretty sexy and was grateful to have been pushed to try something I never would have done on my own.

The show's fashion expert reconstructed my wedding dress into a sexy one-piece jumper short. I felt like a pop star wearing it as I cut up the remnants in the studio salon for the photo shoot. It was the perfect setting to say good riddance to Max.

I held my head high and took a deep breath. I was 30 years old and more than ready to check the baggage of my 20s, send it on a one-way trip to the past and jetstart my destiny.

With the spotlight shining on the stage of my life, I shredded all of the bottled up feelings of sadness, disappointment and failure that resulted from my divorce. Emotions ran rampant. My heart broke as I cut the fabric of my dress. Worn on the day I felt the most beautiful, it ended up making my life ugly. The garment was supposed to represent my happily ever after. It was supposed to lead me to a loving and supportive husband, a house that smelled like fresh-baked sugar cookies upon entering, and a white picket fence lining a backyard in which my husband and I would read newspapers and eat breakfast on Sunday mornings while the dogs ran around and children played. Instead, it left me a victim of deceit, feeling empty, lost and scared.

With every cut into that couture Greek thread, I reclaimed my dignity. I made peace with the fact that my mother spent thousands of dollars on my wasted wedding, that I can't look back on that day and smile, or hang up those photos of myself with family and friends.

Up until recently, I thought I wasted the most important years of my life on Max. But while tearing that fabric apart with clenched fists, I forgave myself and began to heal. Sure, I have scars. But that's OK because they made me who I am today.

I'm thankful for the venom. This mid-mid-life crisis may have shattered life as I knew it, but not my life as it is meant to be. Now, even on the most dismal of days, I look outside the window and see a clear blue sky.

With my dress trashed (though not the final time, but more about that later), I was finally 100 percent free of Max. As Ajnira, my spiritual healer, advised, I had become the heroine in the novel of my life. I survived the aftermath of an earth-shattering disaster: divorce in my 20s.

It was now my self-assigned duty to tell the stories of others who had emerged from the rubble, picked the sticks and stones out of their wounds and healed. My story is just one of many from women who survived young divorce. I have been privileged to meet others who came forward to share their experiences of heartbreak and triumph for this book. Together, we will inspire and guide young women whose lives are just about to enter a state of emergency.

Six

Forming the Pack

Young divorced women are like shelter dogs. You know they exist, but you don't realize how many there actually are until you meet one. Then, you realize they're everywhere. Some dogs end up at pet rescues because they were suddenly abandoned by the ones they loved, others because they were removed from unhealthy situations. With life as they knew it gone, these dogs are left alone with their thoughts, fears, and hope for the future: finding a new companion to share their over-abundance of love. Shelter dogs, like young divorcées, are survivors. Some rehabilitation may be necessary, but those with good hearts will help them heal. The dogs never forget their pasts, but once they feel safe and confident again, they run through life with wagging tails.

When I first started conducting interviews for this book, I was pretty sure I would have to scour the bowels of the Internet to unearth twenty-something divorced women. Word of mouth and a bit of DIY marketing brought me a few willing participants. I was thrilled when five girls joined my pack. Then, something crazy happened. I wrote a blog for a major news website which examined the reasons twenty-somethings got hitched when they should've ditched, and hundreds of emails flooded my inbox.

I was overwhelmed yet selfishly ecstatic to discover that so many others related to my situation. Through the interviews, launching a subsequent private online support group on Facebook and hosting local meet-ups, I have learned that there are surprisingly common reasons why we not only got married, but also why we got divorced, and that we share similar post-divorce fears.

Through my research and experience, I have concluded that the underlying motivation behind marriage for most women who have gotten divorced is one of the following reasons:

- It was convenient and they followed society-imposed norms of marriage by a certain age.
- A previous relationship left them heartbroken and they figured they'd never again experience a love so deep so they stopped searching and settled for being content.
- They'd hoped marriage would change the relationship or their partner.
- They had low self-esteem and didn't think they could do any better.
- Their religious families forced marriage.

Here's why some of the participants got hitched:

Madison, a 29-year-old accountant from New Jersey, admitted to marrying at age 25 even though she didn't feel "crazy love," because she was "content and secure" after a past relationship smashed her heart into pieces. Justifying her decision, Madison said, "We were both financially stable and could have a good life. I felt I would never be hurt by him as long as I didn't give my whole heart."

Maxie, a 28-year-old grad student from California, was drawn to her ex-husband when she met him at age 23 because they both loved music, worked as nurses, had a strained relationship with one parent and loved their dogs. "I think the electricity between us and the fact that we fit well together as a couple united us," summarized Maxie.

On par with major life goals, including a cozy home, babies, and an RV to retire in, Maxie and her man had their future mapped out when she married him at age 26. "Ironically, a couple weeks before he left me, I was talking to my friends about how I am pretty practical and not one to get caught up in romance or naiveté but I felt like I could honestly say that he would never do anything to hurt me and that we had the type of marriage that could weather anything. I had such confidence that I had something special that not too many other people had and that it was unshakeable. Little did I know..." she recounted.

While Maxie went into marriage envisioning a picture perfect future, 28-year-old teaching assistant Brooke from Wisconsin admitted, "I had considered calling it off. But because we had already paid for the hall and booked everything, and I had the dress, the girls had their dresses, etc., I just didn't know how to call it off. For whatever reason, I thought it was going to be easier to go ahead with it all than to stop it. What a silly, young, naïve girl I was."

Similarly, Scarlett, a 29-year-old marketing guru from Toronto, Canada, got married at age 24 thinking of it as her first, never as her only, marriage. "I don't really believe in marriage and forever love, and I don't know that I ever have," revealed Scarlett. She continued, "That could be one of the reasons that I try so hard to protect myself—because I feel like it is inevitable that it will end and I will be hurt."

Scarlett was actually the one who decided to end her marriage. "The biggest disappointment for me was that I couldn't be happy even though I had everything that I'd ever wanted. I had the perfect life, perfect husband, perfect job and everyone else wanted what I had, but it still didn't make me happy."

She told me, "I felt like getting a divorce was the only way that I could fix myself and maybe find happiness in my life."

Rory, a 30-year-old patent examiner from Massachusetts also had marital reservations. She confided, "I thought we were wrong for each other, I thought he would never stop lying and gaslighting me (Let me save you an Internet search: gaslighting is a form of psychological abuse in which false information is presented with the intent of making a victim doubt his or her own memory and perception), and I was afraid that I would always be the breadwinner. I ignored every single worry and doubt; rationalized them away one by one and told myself that my fears were 'normal.' I was afraid to go through leaving him—again. I didn't want to deal with the heartbreak and the reality of a failed relationship. I was scared of being in my late 20s without having captured the American dream. I thought he was the best that I could do and didn't believe I deserved more."

Lack of self-confidence was a deciding factor for other divorcées to marry. Kate, a 30-year-old technical assistant from Connecticut got engaged to her high-school sweet heart at age 20, because, "We were such good friends and had been together for so long, it just seemed natural that the next step was to get married."

However, when they married one year later, Kate had second thoughts. "As I walked down the aisle for a moment I thought to myself, 'I am marrying him because I know I will never do any better.'" She struggled with body image, self-esteem and depression all through middle and high school.

Jackie, 26, from Pennsylvania, experienced a situation similar to Kate's. She said, "I struggled with anorexia and bulimia as a teenager. I was always very self-critical and sensitive as a child, and I had low self-esteem for many years. Some of those traits influenced my decision to marry my ex-husband, as I never realized I deserved better treatment than he ever gave me."

Jackie's divorce was in progress at the time of our interview, but 36-year-old Patricia from Massachusetts is a veteran and knows the struggles Jackie is facing. Of her marriage at age 22, Patricia recalled, "I was insecure, plain and simple. I picked a man who couldn't really hurt me. He was a nice guy from a nice family with nice friends. He was very into me and that was enough for me. I had no idea who I was, why I had picked jerks before, and that an identity couldn't be given to you by someone: I had to carve one myself." Patricia did end up carving her own identity by earning a Ph.D. (that's Dr. Patricia Leavy now!), becoming a women's studies expert and authoring books including *Low-Fat Love*.

If only Sydney, a senior online news editor in Florida, had Dr. Patricia Leavy's advice to consider prior to her own marriage at age 20. "I had no goals in life," shared Sydney. "All of my goals had been shot down, one after the other, so instead I aligned my goals with his, even though I wasn't much interested in them. It was the easiest way to feel like I was actually doing something worthwhile. When I did finally go back to college (I had dropped out to be with him) I had to deal with his jokes about journalism school, how the only gainful employment I'd find was writing obituaries."

Ana, a publisher from the Philippines who married at age 26, told me, "I knew the person was not right for me, but I thought to myself, 'this will do.' I wish I had enough sense of my own self-worth and confidence to know that I deserved better than 'this will do' in anything—not just as a partner, but also as a person. In hindsight, when you know who you are, what you are capable of, you don't simply settle. You make better, wiser decisions. Basically, I should have asked for a marriage, rather than a wedding. That is the difference between a lifetime and a day, a love affair and a relationship."

Social media manager Paige, now 34, gave up goals when she married in her 20s. "I come from a very small town where we all basically marry young. It was the easiest way to get out of Dodge," explained Paige of her hometown in the state of Georgia.

Paige married young at her own will, however, many twenty-something divorcées faced pressure from their families and religious organizations.

Avery, a 27-year-old research assistant in Ohio, told me, "Part of the reason why we got married so soon was because we moved in together about five months after we first met. We were very involved in the church and our youth pastor was encouraging us to get married so we wouldn't set a bad example to the youth we were leading. They all looked up to us. My rationale was, 'I love this man and want to grow old with him.' We stopped having sex after we got engaged and perhaps this was a motivating factor that brought him to want to tie the knot so early."

Willow, an online editor from New Jersey, had a similar situation: "My mother brought it up after she found out we were sleeping together. She was a born-again Christian and said we needed to get married to make it right. He was all for it and proposed that Christmas day." Willow's marriage began when she was 20 years old and ended when she was merely 23. Thanks, Mom.

Over in Arizona, Harper, now 30, found herself in a very controlling religion that was based on dating only with the intent of marriage. Making things even harder, Harper enlightened, "The religion we were in did not permit a 'scriptural divorce' unless adultery was an issue. In leaving him, I also left the religion, which ended relationships with my family as well as his—their choices, not mine. To this day, religion continues to play a factor in how he treats me."

Grace, a 28-year-old grad student from Pennsylvania, also blamed religion for rushing her into marriage. "We went to a conservative Bible college, so it was more of a courtship than dating," listed Grace of factor number one. "There is such pressure in conservative Christian culture to become serious too fast and to fast-track it to marriage. There is no time to consider whether you even want to get married young. Rather, that is presented as the ideal to which one should aspire."

Grace continued, "Like good conservative Christians, we waited to have sex until our wedding night, though I was not a virgin when we got married. Looking back, I think it would have helped if we had lived together or had at least had sex. I think the waiting for sex thing really puts a lot of pressure on relationships. Perhaps we would not have gotten married so young if we were having sex, which would have perhaps given us more time to realize we were not right for each other."

New York travel agent, Elizabeth, 29, discussed how her culture imposed on her to marry her abuser. "I'm Chinese with Christian parents who are from Hong Kong. When I was engaged, I thought that the physical and emotional abuse would go away and he wouldn't do that to me once we were married."

Though her gut told her to call off the wedding, the arrangements were made and Elizabeth feared a backlash from the Chinese community. "In the Chinese culture, face is everything. I didn't want to lose face to my family and myself. Also, I didn't want to leave college unmarried and be called an old maid, even though I was only 23-years-old. In the college that I went to, everyone married young—before they graduated. So I pressured myself into getting married."

While Elizabeth forced herself to meet expectations, Nora, a 27-year-old family law attorney from North Carolina, acknowledged she nudged her boyfriend to propose, though not deliberately. "We'd been fighting a lot and I kept bitching about how he needed to grow up, get a job outside of the house, do things that showed me he was committed to the new state we'd just moved to and was committed to having a great life with me," she began. "We had poor communication and somehow things got confused and he thought I was begging for the proposal. I think he mostly did it to shush my nagging. I mostly said 'yes' because how could I say 'no' to a nice ring and a stable man? That's what you do, right? You say 'yes' when homeboy pulls out the yellow diamond you love."

Scarlett from Toronto also admitted to being swept away by the wedding fantasy. "I always wanted to get married for the wrong reasons—jewelry, the dress, and being able to check it off my life's list of to-dos. I always said that I wanted to be married before 25."

Cherie, a 30-year-old behavioral therapist from California, knows she forced her boyfriend into marriage. "He did not really want to, it's hard to admit that! It makes me seem like a dumbass. Some people will probably think 'Hey crazypants, if you knew he didn't want to get married, then why did you marry him?' But let me tell you, I loved this man. I can't explain it." Parental pressure eventually led to a laid back proposal.

"The word 'proposal' isn't quite the correct word for what it was," noted Cherie. "We were in a drive-thru ATM and as he was pulling out cash he said 'Dude, let's just do it, let's get married so they back off.' There was no ring, no down on one knee, or 'I love you.' He called me 'dude.'" She added, "My parents bought the ring the next week."

Carly, on the other hand, described a whirlwind romance. Now a 27-year-old law student from New Hampshire, Carly got married five years ago to a man she met at San Lorenzo Market in Florence, Italy. "After our second date, which was also his birthday, he asked me to marry him and I laughed. I said 'no.' He asked a bunch of times, and one night he asked and it was such a perfect moment that I said 'yes.'"

Carly was attracted to her man's sense of adventure and humor. "There was never a dull moment in our relationship before we got married, and I love someone who is as spur-of-the-moment as I am." Yet, Carly came clean with herself on the day of her wedding. "I kept looking to see if my ex-boyfriend was there. I think I got married in part to get back at him for how awful the end of our relationship was," she confessed.

Lily, a 29-year-old social worker from Virgina, married her high school sweetheart. "I either get the 'Aw, you married your high school sweetheart?' gooey response, or the 'You married the first person you slept with?' incredulous response. And secretly I myself could not definitively decide what I believed," shared Lily.

Of course she loved her husband, but Lily said, "A nagging, out of focus part of me always wondered if I had settled down too early. Could I really have found the right person when I was still basically a child? Movies and magazines led me to believe it was perfectly reasonable that I would fall in perpetual love at 17, but logic and statistics begged to differ. Of all the people in the world, what are the odds I found the right person so early?"

It turns out neither Lily, nor any of the participants in this book, found "the one" in their first husbands. While every marriage suffered the same demise, the underlying reasons for divorce vary. And some are quite disturbing, as you'll find out next.

Seven

Here Comes the Divorcée

When a twenty-something woman's marriage is officially declared dead, she must journey through six levels of reality before reaching the after-life, also known as the 'Celebration' phase. I've found the levels to be as follows:

- Relief
- Devastation
- Failure
- Embarrassment
- Anxiety
- Anger
- Celebration

Relief: For a brief moment, a sense of calm floats across the woman's mind as she realizes that she will no longer have to deal with the stress of her marriage.

Devastation: Shortly after the 'Relief' phase, reality hits. The woman faces the fact that her marriage is over—finito, done, adiós—and her whole life is falling apart.

Failure: In the days following her divorce declaration, the woman names herself the only twenty-something divorcée in the world. She's blames herself for getting married, wonders if she tried hard enough to make things work and is convinced she's a failure.

Embarrassment: Dread overcomes the woman as she faces the fact that she's going to have to update her social networking page's relationship status. She believes everyone she went to high school with is going to judge and consider her a failure, as well. The woman edits her profile and quickly removes the automatic update posted on her wall. Then, she stresses out about how to tell her extended family. (Tip: A therapist once told me she suggests the phrase, "I'm happy to announce my divorce.")

Anxiety: The woman begins to freak out. Not only is her marriage over, but also she is single, most likely for the first time in years. All of her friends seem to be in serious relationships and she must re-learn how to date and decode guy language. She wonders, "Does the three-day rule still apply these days? What is sexting? Why don't men just pick up the phone!?"

In addition to those worries, the woman lies awake all night telling herself she is never going to have children (or siblings for her current children) because she'll be too old by the time she falls in love again *if* she even re-marries! Will her new man care that she is divorced? How will she explain that on dates? These questions shoot out of a young divorcée's mind like an automatic weapon.

Anger: Sadness is oceans away at this point. The woman is furious with herself for marrying "that asshole" and even more furious with the "asshole" for putting her through all his actions, assuming he is the one behind the marriage's demise. During the anger phase, the woman vows to move on with her life, as challenging as it may be at the time. Living well will be her best revenge.

Celebration: The days of sighing and crying are long past. Maybe the nights once spent tossing and turning between the sheets now happen with a new, better man. Or perhaps, the woman isn't even sleeping under sheets because she's on an exotic island vacationing with her best girl friends and there's no time to rest. The point is that she's looking forward, having reached a place where she is at peace with the state of her life and she's making the most of every new day.

The six steps of this difficult journey may vary, but the road traveled unites each woman.

Examining the reasons why young marriages end, I asked participants of this book to cite their main sources of discord.

Common themes include:

- Addiction: drugs, gambling, pornography
- Goals changed or were not discussed
- Lack of support towards career goals
- Absence of passion
- Physical and emotional abuse
- Disagreement on wanting children
- Infidelity

Participants discuss why they ditched:

Let's jump right into things with perhaps the most surprising cause of divorce among women in their 20s: porn.

Mae, a 28-year-old managed-accounts specialist from Massachusetts, discovered that her husband was actually married to porn. "Often he chose to forego having sex with me for his pictures," she revealed. "I actually walked in on him one time. The pain and anger I felt was indescribable. It felt like a bullet through my heart."

Rory, the patent examiner from Massachusetts, dealt with the same issue. "When I began to suspect that he was cheating on me while I was pregnant, I started fishing around for evidence. That's when I discovered the porn. Not that he looked at it from time to time, but that he was obsessed with it; pornography addiction to the nines. That was the beginning of the end right there."

Rory continued, "Each time, he promised it wouldn't happen anymore, he didn't do it that often and it wasn't an obsession. He said it wouldn't impact me anymore and our own intimacy would get better. The lies and broken promises go on and on."

She later found out he viewed porn on his cell phone on the train to work and while at work, but it doesn't stop there. "He paid for it behind my back with credit cards I didn't know about. When I found out that much, I stopped trying to uncover his habits and instead started planning my escape from the hell that I was in. It was over at that point and I didn't want to know any more. The uncovering of a dirty spooge-rag found under our sofa was like the white surrender flag going up on my ability to handle the bullshit anymore."

Lucy, a 26-year-old claims adjuster from Texas is part of the "I Married a Porn Addict" club. However, her story ended with a stomach churning twist. She began, "After about of year of marriage I noticed that my ex did not get aroused by normal methods. He didn't want foreplay, but instead wanted me to pose in compromising positions." She thought to herself, "No worries, we can all get kinky sometimes."

Then, one night after they made love, Lucy awoke to find her husband was not beside her in bed, or anywhere in their apartment. She noticed the front door slightly ajar and spotted her husband making his way around the corner. "Something told me to check the phone and dial *69," she informed. "I always had intuition that never steered me wrong, unless of course I ignored it. That night I didn't ignore my gut, and *69ed the phone. To my surprise, it was a chat line—a phone chat line for men to meet men!"

Lucy put on her robe and trailed her husband. To her disgust, she found him around the corner with another man! "He was getting up from his knees and the other was adjusting his pants. It took everything in me not to scream. Even to this day I want to vomit."

After her husband returned home, Lucy confronted him. He blamed it on his mental illness, which was major depression. Lucy left that night.

Porn addition is one issue I didn't expect to hear participants discuss. But I did anticipate stories such as those from Maureen, an attorney from Oregon who signed divorce papers at age 29 because she and her spouse each changed goals. "I guess we discussed them, but at 23 I didn't really even know what my goals were," she let me know.

Maureen accomplished her career goal, but her husband didn't follow her mature path. "Three days before I announced I was leaving, I had lost a big trial at work. I called him and asked what we were going to do that night. I had been working 15 hours a day for three weeks and was heartbroken about losing my trial. He told me he was taking a road trip with a friend to go buy a kegerator. I just sat in the living room and cried for hours that night. I knew I had to leave."

She elaborated on their relationship: "He was always trying to touch me and be intimate and I didn't want it at all. He insisted that I was 'broken' and should go to a doctor to see why I didn't want to have sex." However, Maureen explained, "I just wasn't attracted to him and felt like he was my kid instead of my husband."

Hadley, a marketing coordinator from New York, married at age 25 hoping it would make her guy more responsible. "I paid the bills and had to push and beg for him to at least help me with house projects. I hoped that we'd act like real adults like our friends that were beginning to have families. Instead it was more of a frat house situation."

Hadley's husband gambled away their future while she yearned to get financially stable. "He didn't seem to care, living paycheck to paycheck was just fine for him."

Like Hadley, Alexandra, a now 30-year-old attorney from Texas, married a man who didn't have ambition to move up in the world. "He was satisfied living in a low-income apartment complex and having a job rather than career. I wanted a home with a yard and needed a partner with earning capacity to help me shoulder the financial burden of having a family," she told me.

Alexandra hoped with a more serious commitment, her other half would put forth more effort. "You would think I would be more logical considering I'm an attorney, but when it comes to emotions, we're all at risk for making poor decisions," she stated.

Alexandra reflected, "Everything had just been so rushed, and I think now, 'For what? Because I wanted for this, so badly, to be love? Because I wanted to be married with children before 30?'"

Avery from Ohio should introduce her ex-husband to Alexandra and Hadley's. She shared, "I wanted to pursue a graduate degree and dreamt of success in the medical field while he just wanted peace and happiness. He sought simplicity and was satisfied with having little. He agreed that he would go to school and get a college degree but he could never complete a course nor maintain a steady job."

Earlier I introduced you to Harper, who married because of her strict religion. Surprisingly, that's not the main factor behind her divorce. It was because her husband didn't allow her to pursue her dreams. After four years of marriage, Harper divorced at age 26. "I was tired of being controlled and manipulated, and realized that he had molded me into what he wanted in a wife, but I wasn't who I wanted to be as a person. I was miserable, depressed, and not really a great mom to my son at that time, because I wasn't happy. Even if he had agreed to go to counseling with me, I think we would have ultimately divorced, because I wanted to grow as a person, and he didn't want to allow it, or grow with me."

What happens when a couple is on the same goal line but one scores and the other doesn't? Liz, a 27-year-old MBA from Massachusetts knows the answer.

Liz emailed me, "When we starting dating up until right before things got rough, we totally had the same goals. We both wanted a home and a family. When we graduated, he with his master's and I with my undergrad, we were excited to move to Dallas and get started. He took a job that turned out to be a terrible job, whereas I got a dream job. I was traveling, planning events, and taking clients out to fancy dinners. He was selling copiers. That is when I think we started not communicating. I think that it really bothered him that a kid without her master's degree was making more money than he was. I think that is where the tension started."

But then, the tables turned big time. "When he got his new job, he was all over the globe for weeks at a time. While I was at home wondering what country my husband was in, he was in bars racking up crazy tabs without a care in the world. He would go days without calling, texting or emailing, not even letting me know if he made it safely," said Liz. "He was getting power and starting to see that having a wife in the States was holding him back."

Thirty-year-old Monica from Hong Kong thought she and her husband were on the same page when she married him at age 24. "I thought he would go on a great big life adventure with me, but it turned out all he wanted to do is, metaphorically, sit on the couch and watch TV every night," recounted Monica.

She filed for separation after five years of marriage and cited, "I had a lot of dreams and aspirations. He was a simple guy who just wanted a wife and kids. Mostly he thought that I was just dreaming and said 'yes' to anything I wanted to do in the future. I didn't realize he didn't actually think that I was serious about wanting to work overseas, taking a six month break to travel the world and go on a volunteer project in Africa."

Like Monica, Brooke, the 28-year-old teaching assistant, discussed life goals before walking down the aisle. Though Brooke and her husband had similar plans, things shifted following the wedding. Several years of continual shifting caused the pair to completely drift apart.

Brooke described her ex-husband as being "more like a robot than a person." She elaborated, "He didn't need emotional connections in his world in order to survive. Our relationship was more like that of coworkers than husband and wife."

That said, sex was an issue: "He wanted it, a lot," mentioned Brooke. "But because he was totally incapable of giving me the emotional support and connection that I needed, he got very little of it."

Jezabelle, a 24-year-old inside sales rep from New York, married her polar opposite. While she calculated every turn, her husband was content riding on cruise control. "I'm a very driven person, always wanting to accomplish the next goal, whereas he was quite complacent with how things were and therefore had no motivation. The longer we were together the less motivated he became—in part because he saw I was willing to do anything to take care of us," she shared.

Pre-marriage, Jezabelle said, "He wasn't working, he was complaining all the time about me being so busy. I worked multiple jobs so that we could afford to live nicely and go out. Yet, he was miserable because we lived so far from his friends and family. Keep in mind, he voluntarily moved near me when we started dating because I was still in school. Between school and my sorority, I wasn't going to have much time to drive out to see him. He didn't have a car to drive to see me and was very paranoid about me cheating and not being home a lot." Of course, dreams of her husband changing after marriage never came to fruition.

Across the world, Sara, a 28-year-old musician from Egypt, had a revolutionary divorce. In the beginning, Sara and her love were two peas in a pod. However, "It was just him making it seem that way," observed Sara. "He said that like me, he was open minded, liberal, a rebel, non-traditional, and not too family oriented. Unfortunately in the end, my job, music, and master's degree were intimidating him and I wasn't spending enough time taking care of him, according to him."

The Egyptian Revolution on Jan 25, 2011 brought forth a wake up call. She played it back: "My ex was on a business trip all of December and January. He even missed my birthday. A few days after, the Revolution happened. All phone lines and Internet were cut, as we were blacked out from the whole world. Overnight, the streets became chaos, as police, thugs and innocent people were killed. When the phone lines started working again, my parents called to check up on me. When I called my husband a day later fuming that he didn't ask about me, his response was, 'Your parents said you were fine.'"

That was just the first sign for Sara. She continued, "All travel to Egypt was stopped until the streets became safe again. So he came back in early February. I begged my manager at work to send me on a trip because I couldn't stand being with him and I left in March. I recognized that I was miserable and was complaining to everyone. I realized that the Revolution was about people who had been oppressed for 30 years and here they were fighting for their freedom, risking their lives. Why couldn't I?"

Sara began saving up, while expecting the worse. She feared losing her home and disownment by her parents. "There is not a single divorced person in our family. I had no precedent, and no idea what to expect."

Sara took a risk by ending her marriage, but for others, the risky situation *was* their marriage. These are the women who survived abusive husbands.

Bethany, a 28-year-old nonprofit employee in Ohio, declared, "My ex was the first man who ever put his hands on me and he'll be the last. 'Til death do us part' was not going to be my own, at his hands."

Bethany courageously opened up, "My husband had taken to hitting, choking and biting me. In addition to verbally abusing me, he also controlled every aspect of my life. Thankfully, through a series of ninja-type secret financial moves, I broke free from him, went on to get a master's degree and found a wonderful job."

She acknowledged, "Abuse is not an action/reaction thing. Abuse comes from the inside of an abusive person. There was nothing I could do to start or stop the abuse. He would get mad and hit me even if I was completely silent. It was a decision that he would have to make and he seemed unwilling to take complete blame for the violence. That's why I decided to proceed with the divorce."

Sydney from Florida was "Sorry to say that I came away from many fights with black eyes and split lips." She said, "I inflicted my own share of damage in my attempts to fight back and defend myself. At the time, I held myself equally responsible for the physical nature of our fights but in retrospect I realize that I was only like this with him, and only because he went there first."

Unfortunately, drugs played a heavy role in Sydney's life at the time. She recalls one fight in particular: "He ended up sitting on me, punching me in the face over and over again while I was screaming for him to stop. I still remember how dark and empty his eyes looked, how I was sure that was going to be the end of my life. Suddenly his eyes changed from rage to horror, and he scrambled away crying, saying he was sorry over and over again. I went into the bathroom, and when I saw my face I had to brace myself against the counter. He had given me two black eyes and a bloody lip, and my neck was ringed in broken capillaries. There was no way around it—he had beaten me up. It was awful, and I wanted to die from shame," she pronounced.

Over in Virginia, 23-year-old Riley was battling an alcoholic husband. Of one incident, she said, "His alarm went off at 4:00 a.m. because he had to be at work. I tried to wake him up because he absolutely couldn't be late. I even tried to push him out of bed. But, because he was still drunk, this completely set him off and he called me every bad name he could think of. He told me I was fat, ugly, stupid, lazy, worthless, etc., and began beating me over the head with his pillow."

Riley continued, "In self-defense, I punched him in the chest and immediately knew I made a stupid decision. He threw me down on the bed, wrapped his hands around my throat, and said 'I want to hurt you so fucking bad right now.' We both kind of looked at each other and knew that was it, he had crossed the line."

Fiona, a 29-year-old kindergarten teacher from Maryland, discussed the bipolar relationship she had with her husband. "The highs were the best times ever and the lows were scary and miserable."

Whereas Fiona wanted to resolve conflict, she said her ex-husband "wanted to avoid me and threatened divorce." She revealed, "He later resorted to drugs, alcohol, gambling, and avoiding our family."

Fiona was almost seven months pregnant when her husband threw her across the kitchen. Another incident occurred when their son was ten months old. "He held me down on our bed and strangled me, trying to kill me," Fiona disclosed. "That is when I got a restraining order and we separated for good."

Prior to that, she noted, "His drinking and drug use had gotten out of control. He was passing out in our home, showing up late, avoiding everyone in our family, and blowing through thousands of dollars on drugs, gambling, TVs, trips and boxing tickets."

Fiona recalled another abusive night: "We went out to celebrate my birthday and instead of staying home after dinner with me, he insisted on going to the bar. I stayed home with our infant son. He came home hammered and I confronted him about his drinking and drug use and how it was affecting our family. He screamed at me, which was a regular occurrence, and then held me down on the bed strangling me. I called the cops and he fled the scene."

Molly, an engineer from Massachusetts who married when she was 26 years old, became a victim of her husband's hand while attending a friend's tropical destination wedding. "We had been drinking and got into a fight about something I can't remember on the walk back to the hotel room," she recounted. "He shoved me and I fell to the ground and my heel fell off. I ended up cutting the bottom of my foot so badly on a rock that if we were in the States I would have gone to see if I needed stitches."

Molly's husband was also cheating on her with a woman who worked at their dentist's office, but she didn't let this broad get away with being a home-wrecker. And get this—her mother-in-law at the time came with her for emotional support!

Molly painted a picture of the scene: "I had an appointment the week after I found out he was cheating on me with her. Rather than cancel, I went in with my head held high, standing next to his mother. I saw the woman in the background of the receptionist chair and as calmly as I could, I extended my hand and said, 'Excuse me? I believe you recently became an acquaintance of my husband,' loud enough for all her coworkers to hear. I was hoping they would all realize what she had done without causing a complete scene."

Thus, Molly shook the hand of the woman who destroyed her life. "My heart beat so hard I thought I was going to pass out. She looked like she ran into a back bathroom and vomited after that encounter."

Full-time grad student Leanne's husband also strayed from their marriage. The 27-year-old from New Mexico attributed it to her busy schedule and his coworker. "I started to volunteer with an animal shelter and this work consumed most of my time. We barely spent any time together and lived like two passing ships. Then, he met a new employee at work. She was extroverted, friendly, attractive and creative. We both liked her and spent lots of time with the woman and her boyfriend." And I bet you can guess what happened next in that situation.

Let's quickly go back to substance abuse, which I found to play a role in the divorces of many abused women. However, not all the women who married addicts were physically abused. Remember

Lily, the woman who married her high school sweetheart? He became a coke-head.

"We met in a park near our home in Virginia after work one day, per his request, so he could tell me he wasn't sure he wanted to be married to me anymore," said Lily. "He wanted to start marriage therapy, he said, but he would be moving to his parents' home that night. I went home and collapsed, devastated."

She called a good friend who lived nearby and came rushing to her side. Lily told me, "I wasn't at all prepared for what she had to say. She had learned a week before that my husband had been doing cocaine and he might even have a drug problem. I realized I really didn't know him at all at that moment, I didn't know our marriage. There's nothing more dramatic than learning that the person you are most intimate with has been lying to you. It shook me to my very core."

Some people change behind your back, others in front of your face. That was the case for Gwen, a high school English teacher in Michigan who married at age 24 and was divorced by 26. She explained, "As our relationship went on, we both became vegans, environmentalists, and had tons in common politically, but eventually things sort of diverged. He got less religious and his political ideas became more extreme."

The change actually led Gwen to have an affair. She's not the only participant to do so, but I can say that from my conversations, everyone who did explore other options acted because something was lacking in their marriage.

Most couples marry to start a family. But not every woman has maternal instincts. What happens when a family man falls in love with one of those women?

Maxie from California divorced after marrying at age 26 because of her stance on motherhood. She said, "I'm not exactly the maternal type with children over the age of six. I love, love, love babies, but kids and teens, not so much." Feeling horrible, she continued, "That distaste, paired with the fact that I had yet to finish school or establish a career when we were married made me fearful of getting pregnant and having a baby before we were ready. The very idea seemed like it would be life shattering because I have a tendency to worry about things I cannot control."

There was an underlying reason for Maxie's feelings however, which makes total sense. "I grew up with a single mother who became pregnant with me by accident and struggled. For Godsakes, of course it freaked me out. As such, I had voiced a few times that the idea of children terrified me and that I wasn't sure if I would be good at it. So naturally, I was fearful and on the fence. I told him I'd be OK with just him and no kids."

At that time, Maxie's husband agreed to it because he just wanted her to be happy. But ultimately, it led to the end of their relationship. Maxie provided insight: "All of a sudden he had been thinking about how he shouldn't be with me because I wouldn't love our children because I would only be having them for him. Shame on me for telling him I thought he was put on this earth to be an amazing daddy and that he would be a natural at it, whereas I would have to work on being a parent. Why did he interpret that so harshly, like I'd only be doing it begrudgingly for him and that I would be a terrible mother? Seriously, he told me I would be a terrible mother and that he didn't want to subject his future children to that. Who says that to their life partner and thinks nothing of it?"

Contrary to Maxie, Liv and her ex-husband both wanted children. Then, her husband changed his mind. Liv, who married at age 25 and was divorced by 27, shared, "He told me later that he never wanted children but didn't want to lose me and figured I would grow out of wanting them." Noting the crossed lines of communication, Liv stated the sad fact, "I built a life on a man who didn't actually exist."

Jackie, a 26-year-old scientist from Pennsylvania, can't say she had mixed signals of communication with her ex-husband. But that's only because she didn't have any in the first place. Jackie explained, "We didn't really fight, per se, but looking back I wish we would have, because we never talked about our problems and both of us were very conflict avoidant."

A people-pleaser, Jackie spent most of her relationship tending to her man, while ignoring herself. "This led to few conflicts, but also to feelings of resentment and unfulfilled needs on my end. He claims he was happy with me, but that was probably because I catered to his needs throughout our entire relationship," regretfully informed Jackie.

With conflict never resolved, Jackie internalized her feelings, which later became resentment. "I would blame myself or go somewhere and cry and he would ignore the problem and assume I would just get over it."

In those instances, Jackie's then-husband did try to solve challenges. Unfortunately, those challenges occurred on the TV screen. "He turned to video gaming to avoid communication with me when he didn't want to talk," revealed Jackie.

She's not the only participant who cited this hobby as a problem in her marriage. Some felt that their ex-husband's boy toys ruined the passion in their relationships. "That definitely dwindled when he got very involved with online gaming," shared Jackie. "We did still have some affection like a hug and kiss when we went to and came back from work, and some cuddling, but definitely not passion, per se. He was blatantly not interested in sex anymore, at all."

One participant, Hannah, a freelance writer from North Carolina who married at age 22 and divorced by age 25, told me she actually didn't even discuss key issues like parenthood with her ex-husband prior to getting married. When they did, Hannah found out "We didn't share the same values."

Harlowe, a 30-year-old teacher from Virgina who got engaged at age 24 after only four months of dating, told me, "We had definitely discussed marriage, but mostly in the silly puppy-love, big-dreams kind of discussions. I don't think we ever seriously discussed the long-term implications in a realistic conversation."

Oh, the long-term implications of marrying the wrong partner. Unfortunately, those nagging reminders don't go away after the ink has dried on divorce papers.

Eight

Emotion Sickness

“**N**ow what?”

It's a question that's top of mind for the newly crowned divorcette (AKA divorcée on the prowl) as she realizes she needs to play the hand she's been dealt.

No matter her response, one thing is certain: she's going to freak out. We all at some point or another have a mini nervous breakdown about becoming a party of one and dealing with the struggles that accompany said status.

Below are common things keeping women just like you up all night. Check all that apply.

___ Motherhood: Will I be too old to have children once I find love again?
___ Trusting love: How will I ever be able to give my heart away again without getting hurt?
___ Finances: I'll be paying for my marriage the rest of my life! Or so it seems.

___ Trusting my own judgment: I can't believe I let myself get married to the wrong man. How will I know it's right the next time love comes along? I don't want to be divorced twice!

___ Failure: I'm a loser because I couldn't make my marriage work.

___ Falling behind in life: I'm probably going to have gray hair by the time I meet the real Mr. Right. I'll never be a mother, own a house, or meet other life goals that I've set for myself.

Whether you checked one or every item, rest assured, it gets easier. The timing for me to write this chapter is quite appropriate. Though I've made it through my divorce, I've recently become an onlooker as my best friend's life falls apart.

Remember Penny and how we planned our weddings together? While I was rebuilding my life, Penny was buying a beautiful house with her husband (who was also her first and only boyfriend) and decorating a nursery for their baby. Now, I'm planning her divorce party.

Religious differences were the main factor behind their split. "People keep asking me, 'Didn't you know about this before you got married?'" Penny vented to me. "I'm annoyed more and more every time I'm asked what led me to this point. We talked about our different religions as we were casually dating more than nine years ago, before we got engaged, during the wedding-planning process, and after we got married and were really talking about having kids."

Penny's marriage is a perfect example that major issues won't change after marriage, even if you think you've come up with a way to manage the differences. It got to the point where Penny had to seek professional care and medicate herself to deal with the situation. It eased her decision to leave.

"My life was such a mess and with no one else to turn to, I went to my OBGYN when the baby was just two months old. I didn't feel as though I had post-partum depression, but I knew I wasn't feeling like myself. The doctor talked me through a lot of matters. By the end of the appointment, he told me I was 'a woman living on the edge.'" I left with a prescription and a list of local psychiatrists."

Now drama free I've seen Penny's personality change almost overnight. But that doesn't mean she's not struggling as a newly single mom. One of the first things Penny said to me after she decided to leave her soon-to-be-ex-husband was, "I get it now. I totally get what you have been talking about. I'm 28 years old and I have to start my life over from scratch. I'm happy I have my son, but I wanted him to have a sibling close in age and now that's never going to happen."

Welcome to the club, Penny. Thirty-year-old Alexandra from Texas is a member. "If you thought it was difficult finding your soul mate before, try being divorced and having a small child," Alexandra told me during our interview.

An attorney who met her ex-husband when she was a mere 11 years old, Alexandra admitted, "Not only do men think I've failed at marriage, they're less than enthusiastic to embark on a relationship with a woman who must share her time with a child."

She elaborated, "I'm learning how to balance my daughter's needs against the personal time that I must have in order to be a mentally healthy adult and mom." On top of that, Alexandra said, "I'm still battling with letting go of the pain from the divorce and focusing on living in the present."

Belle, a 25-year-old medical assistant and newly single mama, regretted not doing more to nurture her relationship after the birth of her daughter. "I had school, he had work, and we were surviving off of his income alone. I felt like it was my job to care for and raise my daughter. I regret not taking the initiative to get a sitter and treat him to time out."

Admitting she gave up a piece of herself to care for her family, Belle noted, "I put them at the center of everything I did. I don't have trouble seeing my life on my own. I just never wanted this to happen. I can save my money, pay my bills on time, and I can adapt. Divorce was the one thing I always feared I couldn't handle."

Post-divorce parenting had Fiona from Maryland on edge. "He is trying to be 'Dad of the Year' now and it is a hard pill to swallow when I know the *real* him," she said of her substance abusing ex. "I continue to struggle with understanding why he did this to me and why he can be clean and sober now, but couldn't do jack shit to save our family."

While she was excited to have the opportunity to find herself and someone who will treat her right, Fiona worried, "There aren't many good guys. I have to accept that I might be single forever and I have to be happy with just me and my son."

Naturally, Fiona felt like she was falling behind in life. "Of the five friends who were pregnant at the same time as me, four are pregnant again." However, she realized, "I'm getting a second chance at happiness and unfortunately when 50 percent of my friends' marriages end in divorce, I'll be starting my new, happier life."

Riley from Virginia found dating as a single mother to be a challenge. "I know that a lot of men these days don't mind, but I have had a hard time trying to decide when the 'right' time is to tell a guy that I have a kid. When we first meet? On our first date? After three dates? It's so hard to feel it out. That's why I tend to avoid dating altogether lately," she confessed.

Kate from Connecticut's biggest fear is never meeting anyone to share her journey. "I really want more children but fear it may not be in the cards for me," she said of balancing life as a single mom while working full-time and going back to school to further her career.

If you're like me, you're probably thinking, "Well, at least they had their babies!" See, the majority of young divorcées freak out because they are convinced they lost their chance to ever become a parent.

Hadley from New York divulged, "I fear two things: settling for someone again (even though I tell myself I won't settle for anything less than I deserve) and reaching my late 30s and still not finding Mr. Right and not having children, or having a child alone simply because I want to be a mom someday."

Hadley wasn't afraid to say, "I was struggling with anxiety, mostly over where I am in life at age 29 compared to my friends, but I've recently realized I can't compare myself and my situation to others. While I may be envious of some parts of their lives, they also have other parts that I am glad I don't have to deal with." You hear that, ladies?

However, I'm sure many of you still feel like Chole, a 26-year-old missionary from Texas, who opened up, "I want a happy marriage with babies. I fear that this will never happen. I also fear being 39 and having my first child, not that I wouldn't love or care for a kid if it had issues, but I really don't want to be a parent late in life. My mom was 35 when she had me and there is a definite generation gap that gets in the way sometimes."

Chloe shared, "I wanted to be married young and grow together and support our dreams. I wanted to have kids before I was 30, and I wanted to be married for at least three years before that."

Hearing Rory's story should make those like Chloe feel grateful for their babyless marriages. Rory enlightened, "I'm afraid my son will resent me for the divorce some day. I'm afraid being raised a product of a broken home will harm him for life. I pray that because I left his father when he was so young, he'll never remember life being any different than mommy and daddy living in separate houses and he'll grow up wonderfully with minimal negative impact. But the uncertainty of how he'll perceive the split grips me with fear."

Rory elaborated on divorced parenthood, "I'm also afraid that down the road if he doesn't like how I am raising him, he'll tell me, 'I hate you and I want to go live with my dad!' Just contemplating the potential heartbreak that would cause me hurts my insides. And then I start thinking that I'll be the worst mother ever! Too lax or too giving all because I'm scared that my precious baby boy will grow up and break my heart by choosing his father to live with over me. And then I will have failed at the one thing that means the most to me, and that's being a good mom even when it's hard and the stakes are high. That's the scariest part of my future right there. Failing my son as a mother."

Rory doesn't have the answers for that situation, but when it comes to dating as a divorced mom, she has washed her fears away. "I apparently have 'baggage.' Hogwash. I don't have baggage. I have knowledge, experience, maturity, wisdom, confidence and heart." On a side note, following our interview, Rory met a divorced dad who recognized this, has fallen in love and is having his baby!

Madison from New Jersey also had a baby with her post-divorce boyfriend, but now fears remarrying! "If I ever get married again, I worry about how to do it and if I should make a stink out of it or not."

For now, Madison will focus on her career. "I do have the kid and dog—my baby is my new life. I am with his father, but marriage is not in sight for me at this time."

She's having a hard time trusting love for a third round. Her first fiancé broke up with her over the phone, abruptly stating, "I have cancer and can never see you again." She later learned he entered remission and got married a month before they were supposed to, but to another bride. Her next engagement led to marriage and then divorce, causing Madison to conclude; "Engagements and marriage ruin things."

While Madison blames rites of passage for the ultimate downfall of her relationships, some young divorcées point fingers at themselves for sticking around so long.

Molly from Massachusetts, who was divorced at 28, said "My biggest regret is not being strong enough to make the decision to leave my ex-husband. I regret that he made the final decision for divorce as I was still trying to make it work for fear of what divorce would mean for me—shame, embarrassment, etc. The woman that I am today would have packed up and left the house the very night I found out he was cheating because ultimately I already knew I could never forgive him. My moral obligations, passion for my vows, and fear of what people would think forced me to hang on for longer than I should have, and ultimately the divorce ended up being his call."

Mae said since her divorce, "I struggle with loneliness, and I also struggle with my spirituality. I was raised in a Christian home, but for the last ten years, I have not felt deserving or good enough to call myself a Christian. I am very hard on myself, and while I have goals I wish to accomplish, I hold myself back and seem to always be reaching high, but aiming low. This mostly occurs in my love life."

Over in the Philippines, Ana, the publisher who divorced at age 27 after a year of marriage, feared loneliness after her daughter grew up and moved out of their home. To make matters worse, she had to deal with cultural stigma. "You can't expect to be in a country where there is no divorce and not face hurdles; not go through stereotyping. I have often wondered what it was like for other women in places where divorce is more culturally accepted. I mean, yes, under all circumstances, divorce is a bitch and there is simply no other way around it, but I've often wondered if having divorce available has made people more accepting and understanding of people who have to undergo it."

Ana continued, "I was dismissed as immature, an inconsiderate mother and an unworthy, selfish wife. Women are supposed to hold up half the sky and the whole relationship. In the Philippines, it's common to see martyrs; women who stay and put up with a lot just to stay married." Ana felt morally judged.

Falling in love is a risk well worth the reward, but when that love comes crashing down, learning to trust your instincts again becomes a daily challenge.

Liv from Pennsylvania feared never being able to trust her own decisions. "I was convinced that I was madly in love with my husband and let so many things go unchecked because of what I felt. I'm so afraid that he took my ability to trust in my feelings towards someone else and that I won't be able to really love again," Liv replied to me.

Starting over has made other participants feel like the last girls picked for the team in gym class. Mindi, an art teacher from Pennsylvania who married at age 20 and divorced five years later, shared, "On one hand I thought, 'Wow. I'm only 25 and I'm already divorced. I'm such a loser.' On the other, I thought that I would quickly find love again, and that hasn't happened. So now I'm 27, quickly approaching 30, and I'm not married, having babies, or in a house. It's kind of depressing."

Leanne from New Mexico is in a house, but it's her parents'. She recalled, "I was so fearful that my family would be disappointed in me when I came back home because I felt like a failure. Coming back home and starting over again has made me face my fear of being a loser. I've always been super independent and strived for success. I felt like I didn't need my roots anymore when I was with my ex-husband because we created our own lives."

Leanne informed, "I am in counseling and learning to deal with my anger and sadness. I am learning from my mistakes, facing my fears, meeting new people, accepting my faults and trying to be happy. I am reconnecting with my roots and finding treasures in my history."

That doesn't mean she's forgiven herself, however. "I regret not having the awareness, that it was not going to work out and not having the courage to leave sooner. I regret it ending in such a traumatic way, hurting so many different people."

Starting from scratch is not nearly as appetizing as a homemade cookie recipe. In fact, it leaves many twenty-something divorcées burnt.

Bethany from Ohio told me, "The only thing I really struggle with is being able to trust again—overcoming the fear that a guy will present himself one way and then change drastically in the future."

Lily from Virginia agreed, "I feel like I'm doing really well with everything, but the thought of having to deal with another big-scale rejection is almost paralyzing. And it's a two-part worry:

both that it will happen again, but also that the fear of it will keep me from having a wonderful and fulfilling relationship."

Lily always pictured herself married with children but now doubts marriage as an institution. "I find myself wondering if humans are really meant to couple off and be with one monogamous partner forever. And I'm not sure that's really a bad thing. We change so much as time passes. Is it realistic to think that one person will complement us forever, as we grow and change? In a way, isn't it more reasonable to believe that we would find different people to complement us in different periods of our lives?"

If she does remarry, one thing is certain, Lily has decided she won't be wearing a symbolic ring around her finger. On the contrary, Ariel from New Jersey wants that ring again and it's difficult for her to watch friends live her dream. "I struggle with the fact that everyone around me is now happily engaged or married and having children and I have to start over," admitted Ariel. "It's very hard to see updates on Facebook of engagements and pregnancies while I'm starting from scratch, when I thought I had it all."

Cherie from California feared updating others on her life. "While I was going through this, it seemed everyone else was getting engaged, married, buying houses, having babies, and I was literally back at square one living in my father's basement. One of my biggest fears in deciding to divorce was how to tell everyone and what people would think. I was beyond embarrassed and ashamed, initially."

Jackie from Pennsylvania had to make cutbacks. She pronounced, "Money is tight since I left my husband. Although I have a decent job, it doesn't pay as much as I would hope and he makes a lot of money so I've really had to adjust my shopping habits and lifestyle choices, which is hard."

Jackie added, "I'm also struggling with dealing with judgment from friends about leaving my husband and not giving him a second chance. Many people seem to think I have an obligation to try to work things out because I took marriage vows. I'm still struggling with feeling guilty about hurting him so much and regretful about having gone through with the wedding and then walking out only four months later. Though I feel that I have forgiven him for the disappointment and hurt he caused me, it has been enormously more difficult to forgive myself."

Being alone with your thoughts can be emotionally devastating for a young divorcée. The manifested stress however, also takes a physical toll, even while in the marriage.

Daphne, a 21-year-old customer service rep from Kentucky who married at age 19, says, "I am struggling with my self-image. I gained some weight during my marriage and now I feel like the big, ugly divorced woman. I'm also struggling with being alone. I have not been by myself since I was 16 and it is so hard."

The struggles don't stop once a divorcée finds new love either. We're always reminded of our status. Justine, a New York City public elementary school teacher who married at 25 and divorced by 27, fantasized, "I wish I could have a fresh clean slate with my boyfriend now. I'm tired of hearing 'take your time' and 'be careful.' Trust me, I have learned and I just want people to be happy for me!"

Justine felt like she ruined her wedding experience. "The thought of having to walk into a bridal store again makes me want to vomit. I think weddings are so overrated." She pointed out, "What matters is the marriage, not the wedding. Why do so many of us, including myself, get so caught up?"

Brooke from Wisconsin, who was 23 at the time of her marriage, considers her wedding "a horrible waste." She said, "I regret that others came to the wedding, some traveling from far away, paid to stay somewhere and gave us wonderful gifts. I regret not standing up for my initial fears sooner, faster, more effectively, and ending the engagement so that the wedding never would have happened."

Rory offered food for thought. "I often wonder, did I fail at marriage or did marriage fail me?"

One thing is certain: overcoming emotion sickness begins with self-forgiveness. What's next is up to you.

Nine

Find Your Inner Zen

"I love you."

When those three words just aren't enough to sustain a marriage, a woman must blow them to the wind and welcome another life-changing phrase into her life: "downward facing dog." If a man's best friend is his dog, then a divorced woman's best friend is downward facing dog. I'm referring to yoga. I didn't discover the benefits of this practice until I began writing this book and needed an outlet to burn off anxiety so I could sleep at night (with the help of a little valerian root tea, too!). I wish someone told me to practice yoga during my divorce. Luckily, it's not too late for you!

Ellie, a veteran divorcée, created Meditative Movements (yoga, cardio and strengthening exercise movements combined with affirmations) after she divorced at age 23. She's now in her 50s and here to provide insight for those of you who, like her, married young—she was just 19—and have become a ball of stress and anxiety since your divorce.

"I created my technique as a result of my own healing process," Ellie told me. "The program is about exercising your mind, your body, and your spiritual being in concert so that you can experience life as a confident, loving, and energized individual."

Here's an overview of how the program works. Improvise into your at-home yoga routine:

Centering affirmations such as "I can" and "I listen" are spoken during the warm up; energizing affirmations, "I am loved" and "I am good enough" are stated during the heightened level activity (yoga, cardio, strengthening exercises), and releasing affirmations "I release my need to control" and "I forgive" are said during the cool down phase. Ellie advises to begin your practice with meditation and end with the relaxation portion and the "I know" affirmations.

Ellie explained, "During the divorce process and then the reality of day-to-day living after the divorce, emotions and thoughts tend to be chaotic. I felt afraid, worthless and unlovable. I also felt angry at life because this wasn't supposed to happen to me. Who could I blame? My ex-husband was a good target."

Heed what Ellie told me next: "One thing to note is that by staying angry, you are actually giving your power away and only hurting yourself. It has taken me a while to figure that out."

These exercises allowed Ellie the opportunity to free her emotions and lift angry weight. "Because we are meant to be filled, I could then direct my mind to affirm who I was becoming. Feeling my personal power increase and seeing small healthy outward changes occur kept me following my practice," said Ellie, noting that she also experienced huge successes like quitting smoking and accepting her body. "I changed from only liking my hair to feeling comfortable and sexy in my own skin."

Yoga teaches us to be conscious of every breath, and live in the present. That's exactly what Kelly from New York had to do in order to find peace. "I had my life completely planned out and didn't know what to do when it fell apart," she admitted. "I started seeing a counselor almost immediately and after the initial trauma over the divorce, we focused a lot on living in the present," she shared. "One of the first steps was just recognizing what I was doing and how I was worrying about things that I, or anybody, really, can't control."

Kelly's therapist recommended the following activity, which many divorcées will find helpful: Kelly revealed, "I remember the therapist telling me to imagine a big red stop sign whenever I caught myself having negative thoughts. I instead would refocus to things I was thankful for and current things in my life that were good." She's learned, "Worry really doesn't accomplish anything."

Leanne from New Mexico's healing process included not only yoga and psych sessions, but also a bit of creativity referred to as art therapy.

Here are a few of the projects Leanne's counselor assigned, should you like to explore:

Mold clay—"For anger, I molded clay, hit the clay and drew pictures about how I felt after working with the clay. She also encouraged me to create something beautiful from that clay/anger to transform it."

Draw your dreams—"I've been recording my dreams and drawing them for the last few months," shared Leanne, noting, "that helps me interpret and honor them."

Solve the puzzle—"I drew my story out in a comic book format to get the details down and put the pieces together in my head."

Acknowledging feelings is one part of the recovery process, but expressing them is a whole other ball game. Willow from New Jersey knows. By saying what was on her mind, Willow dug herself out of depression.

"I had a good friend who forced me to go to movies and dinner and it was a start," said Willow. "Then I began dating, something I had never done. I dated a lot and it was fun, but I finally came to a point where I decided to put myself first. I read a lot, including self-help books, and made a commitment to put my feelings and wants first."

She continued, "The new me stopped being a pleaser. She always stays true to herself and isn't afraid to say 'no.' That doesn't mean that I didn't learn to compromise in a relationship and be a better partner—I did, but not at the expense of what I feel is right. I also learned to be proud of where I came from, even though it is a background that is full of addiction, lack of education, and tons of dysfunction. I realized that I made it out and that's a pretty fucking great accomplishment!"

To recap, in this chapter, we explored the importance of finding your inner zen and introduced a few methods to experiment with at your own pace. Now, I present you a little free therapy from Dr. Patricia Leavy, fellow twenty-something divorcée, bestselling author, women's studies expert, and internationally recognized leader in arts-based and qualitative research.

Here are Dr. Patricia Leavy's top three tips for divorced women:

1. **Take some real time to work on yourself.** "Figure out who you are, what you really want, what you enjoy and what your goals are. Sometimes our identities can become entangled with our partner's identity—it can be difficult to discern who in fact you are on your own, what you like and what you don't like," advised Dr. Patricia Leavy. "I think it is especially important to spend time building your professional identity or craft (if you are an artist of some kind, for example). Take concrete steps to work towards your professional goals. It is important to build an identity based on your own activities and accomplishments that no one else is responsible for giving you, nor can anyone else take away. The more 'whole' you become on your own, the more you will have to offer a partner if you do want to find a significant other. Moreover, the more 'whole' you become on your own the less likely you will be to settle for less in a future

relationship. There's no quick hairstyle, makeup, or shopping fix for self-esteem. You need to build it. The more genuine self-esteem you build, the happier you will ultimately be."

2. **Take some time to figure out your role in the breakdown of your relationship.** "It isn't all his fault," noted Dr. Patricia Leavy. "It really isn't. It is vitally important to acknowledge that all relationships are just that, *relationships*. It takes two. Spend some real time thinking about what kind of partner you were, mistakes you made and how you negatively impacted the relationship. A superficial look back won't suffice." She urged, "Dig deep and confront your own role in your failed relationship. This is the only way to grow, find the right partner (if you want to) and become the kind of partner who is likely to have a successful relationship. I have interviewed women in their 50s, 60s and 70s who have been divorced for many years and still do not acknowledge any role in the demise of their relationship other than 'having bad luck with men.' As a result, they do not truly become the best versions of themselves because they are not open to learning the lessons. No matter what he did or who he was, you didn't have bad luck. We all make our own luck. We can remake it too. There's no reason to settle for low-fat love again. As the breakdown of your marriage indicates, there are no substitutes for the real deal."

3. **Spend some time with true girlfriends.** "Be real with them; don't sugarcoat whatever you're going through," prescribed Dr. Patricia Leavy. "We can gather amazing strength from our female friends. Don't settle for false friends. Authentic relationships with other women can provide much needed solidarity, support and humor, which enrich our lives enormously.

Ahh! Breathe in that air! Don't you feel calmer already? You have just been presented with the tools to begin your celebration journey. Now, let's get going.

Ten

Get Out of Town

The adjustment period from bride to un-bethrothed can take an emotional toll on even the most confident of females. Those who leave their home must face the unsettling reality of re-location, whether they move back in with their parents (as I did) or are fortunate enough to afford rent on their own salary. On the contrary, those who remain in their nest are forced to stare at the same memory-filled walls day after day. Of course a fresh new coat of paint can rejuvenate any space, but sometimes you need something a bit more foreign.

Traveling, whether you're hitting the road solo or with your besties, rivals that morning cup o' joe in the ability to invigorate all your days. New sights, sounds, people, and possibilities are just waiting for you to pack your suitcase. Let's face it, you probably got a luggage set at your bridal shower and such an expensive gift deserves to be put to use, right?

When 35-year-old Casey from Florida divorced at 29, she hit the road with her girlfriends. Her destination? Happiness. Casey has led the jet set life ever since and even made a career out it!

"A few months after the divorce was final, I got fired from my job," Casey told me. "So I started a local Girls' Night Out group that met once a month. My girlfriends and I also did Girls Getaways to new destinations. I found this was an unfilled niche in the travel industry and wrote a book, *Girls Getaway Guide to Orlando: Leave Your Baggage at Home.*"

Even if you've been divorced for a while, it's never too late to round up your girls and have some fun in the sun.

Here are Casey's top ten Girlfriend Getaway destinations:

1. **London, England**—"It's the best place to watch the Royal Family and has great shopping. Everyone here speaks English and is very nice!"

2. **Napa Valley, California**—"Napa Valley is where wine tasting is a way of life. Indulge in some of the best wine and most exquisite views you will ever see!"

3. **Montreal, Quebec, Canada**—"A popular destination for festivals, this European-esque city is only a short plane ride from the States, but you will feel as though you are in Europe. And most people are bilingual so you won't have to worry about the language barrier."

4. **Nashville, Tennessee**—"This was the first place I went post-divorce with my girlfriends. Nashville oozes Southern charm with the excitement of music and songwriting."

5. **Key West, Florida**—"Get that island vibe without leaving U.S. soil. Key West's laid back attitude coupled with the exciting Duval Street will ensure you have a fun Girlfriend Getaway—flip flops only; no heels needed."

6. **New Orleans, Louisiana**—"As they say here, 'Let the good times roll.' New Orleans is all about having a good time. You will, too, experiencing everything from their amazing culinary scene to funky stores."

7. **Charleston, South Carolina**—"Look no further than this Southern gem for the ultimate in 'comfort food.' Coupled

with its charm and history, you will fall in love with this fun city."

8. **Palm Beach, Florida**—"Home to some of the nation's wealthiest people, spend a getaway here and you will feel like one of them. From luxurious accommodations to delicious food to exceptional mansions and a beautiful beach, you will love Palm Beach."

9. **Chicago, Illinois**—"A fan favorite in the summer, Chicago is a great place to visit with shows, restaurants, neighborhoods and shopping galore! Catch a Cubs game or indulge in some deep-dish pizza."

10. **The French Riviera**—"The French Riviera is the ultimate in Girlfriend Getaways and where they don't ask if you want wine, they ask what *color* wine you'd like. Get the French Royal treatment in the French Riviera."

While Casey chose to travel with friends, some divorcées prefer to soul search solo. When Harlowe from Virginia divorced at age 27, she treated herself to a divorce vacation to Italy.

Harlowe told me, "My ex and I were supposed to spend our first anniversary on a belated honeymoon trip to Italy. We had already booked the plane tickets for June when things started to fall apart that spring. I decided to keep my ticket, because I had always wanted to visit Italy and needed a good escape from life at that point. June rolled around and my husband filed for divorce officially on our anniversary! It was another sign that I needed this trip to move forward."

However, it wasn't easy. Harlowe recounted, "A few weeks later, I boarded a plane to Switzerland, alone with just a backpack full of summer clothes. I cried the whole way there. I felt lonely, hopeless, and unsure of myself. The train ride into Venice was the same. I felt disoriented and jet-lagged and wondered if I made a huge mistake. I was also in the middle of a job search at home, and felt anxious being out of the country and unavailable for two weeks."

Gradually, the charm and beauty of Italy crept into Harlowe's soul. "In just a day or two, I felt totally at peace with my life, myself, and my travels."

Harlowe summarized the highlights of her European vacation:

The people—"The men in Italy responded well to my newly-single scent, and I enjoyed kissing a few strangers after romantic strolls through cobblestone villages and long, wine-soaked meals under the stars. I spent one evening on the rooftop of a villa with a true Renaissance man, drinking Prosecco and learning the history of the walled city—and feeling so alive I wanted to scream. I also exchanged book recommendations and sob stories with an elderly man on a train."

The serenity—"I took a nap at the top of a mountain near Lake Como, drifting off on a park bench in the breezy sun. It was the best sleep of my life."

The adventure—"I jumped off the cliffs of Cinque Terre into the Ligurian Sea with the most intense sunburn of my life—the bravest move for a girl who is scared to death of heights. I also explored an empty island full of goats."

The culture—"I listened to opera students practice in the background while eating the most delicious spread of meats and cheeses and olives—the soundtrack of relaxation and stimulation at the same time. I rode a bike and a gondola. I ate and ate and ate, soaking up the tastes, knowing I would miss them more than I could ever describe when I left. I snuck into the Galleria dell'Accademia to peek at the statue of David, which took my breath away."

When she returned home, Harlowe told me, "I returned to a job offer and a new city to move to and explore. I never looked back again at my ex-husband. And I still close my eyes and recall moments from that trip that bring the same feelings of independence and satisfaction I experienced that summer."

Violet from New South Wales, Australia didn't just vacation in a foreign country following her divorce at age 26, she moved to one!

She told me, "I moved to London, England because I wanted to have more choices in my life. I knew that in a city like London, I could dress how I wanted, meet people from more cultures, as well as people in the same position as me (moving places) and enjoy the music of a new city!"

Violet also loved the freeing feeling of not knowing anyone. She noted that it allowed her to do and be exactly herself. "I wanted to take the risk, which makes you feel excited and fills you with fear and happiness at once and I like feeling polar emotions! Also, from London I could travel to more cities, as Australia is isolated."

Here's why Violet recommends starting your post-divorce life by moving someplace new:

1. "All of the places you see are not tainted by memories. There are not memories of you and your ex-husband on every street corner!"
2. "There is no chance of accidentally running into your ex-husband or any of his family or friends."
3. "Big cities are full of people who are all displaced and running from their pasts or places, so you meet like-minded people."
4. "Moving to another country means you get too busy to think about your ex-husband and past. You have to find a job, place to live, etc."
5. "Feelings of sadness are replaced by excitement and fear!"
6. "You are exercising courage and so it restores a feeling of being proud and strong."
7. "You will be having too much fun and be too in the present to care about your ex-husband or past."

8. "You have time to learn to love yourself! You are giving yourself time to grow and learn on your own in your 20s, which is important in developing a strong sense of self. That in turn gives you real and deep happiness—much more happiness than a dress and man can ever give you."

9. "You widen your perspective. You realize there is more to life than having a husband and rushing into having children and a mortgage!"

10. "You learn that there are hundreds of other men in the world and that you can take your time to choose one!"

11. "The world is your oyster and an open book. A new country means new opportunities in all areas, including love. Moving to a new country makes you focus on everything in your life, from friends and jobs to boyfriends. It keeps you feeling balanced rather than obsessed with the past."

Convinced? For those considering packing up and shipping out, here are Violet's tips for love and life abroad:

Keep busy! "Planning your move is all-consuming and if you spend your time looking for a job, house, and doing research about the new country, you won't have as much time to be sad or angry about your ex-husband!"

Get involved. "If you move to a new country the world does not come to you, so put yourself out there by going dancing, and joining dating websites and sports clubs. Just get involved and make as many opportunities as possible to meet new friends and a new man! The more openings you make, the more chances you have of meeting others."

Do not contact your ex-husband! "Once you leave, don't email or call your ex. If you do, the positive elements of the relationship might surface and you might start to question your choice to leave. But don't think about going back. You have to remember as much as you are sad or hate your ex-husband, there will always be good aspects too, that can reel you back in. But remember, that does not mean you should go back to him. Leopards don't change their spots and despite the good parts, the bad parts remain!"

Go on a date ASAP! "Don't wait for months to go on a date. I don't mean go and marry someone the next day, I mean just go out and have some male company. This will prevent neuroses from developing and help you to relax. Just go and have a chat. If you stay away from men for too long you might get too scared of them. That's when irrational fears can creep in!"

Do the things you love to do! "It makes you feel free and happy!"

When you do date again, hold back. "Don't jump in and commit. Let a man prove that he is consistent in his behavior by letting him date you for a few months before committing. If a guy is being fake and luring you in at the start with false promises, he won't be able to maintain it for months, so you can see if he is real or not by waiting and taking it slow."

Always be honest with yourself about what you want. "Don't go into a world of denial. Wait for a man that has what you want, and be honest with yourself."

Twenty-six-year-old Chloe was literally on a mission when she left her home state of Texas and moved to Asia to become a volunteer.

Chloe admitted, "The end of my marriage left me broken inside, but also hopeful. For the first time in years I had opportunities in front of me that I could actually take and I embraced them with an open—although a little broken—heart."

In Asia, Chloe was placed working as a paralegal, offering advice and social assistance to female migrant workers.

Chloe shared, "Working with these women, I am constantly amazed by their strength and it gives me heart. Their trials help me put my life into perspective. They leave their families behind—their children, husbands, parents, and siblings—to work as maids and nannies in a society that treats them as second-class citizens. They pay exorbitant fees to employment agencies, and what is left goes to family back home. They send their children to good schools and pay rent for houses they don't live in. When they are mistreated or abused, or simply fired for no good reason, they come to where I work for help. It is humbling. It is heartening. Their strength gives me strength."

Some of these women are also divorced. "In sharing our stories we discover that even though we come from completely different places, we are not so different after all," observed Chloe. "We are not alone, and we can help each other. Serving these women has given me back my confidence and I truly feel like the person I am called to be—something I don't know that I've felt before, especially in my marriage."

Serving others helped Chloe to take the focus off her own messy life and rebuild in a brand new setting. Here, she notes important things to consider for those celebrating their divorce by becoming a missionary on a continent far away from home sweet home:

Listen to your gut. "Going abroad for a year (or any length of time) is a big decision and should not be made lightly. Consider what type of service is right for you. Whether abroad or locally, there are people who need what you have to offer. I heard of my program some years before so I did not have to look too far to find what was right for me. Look for that 'yes!' opportunity, the one that grabs your heart and squeezes. That's where your passion is; take the time to find the opportunity that is right for you."

Focus on your skills. "What do you have to offer? Where can you grow? If you love animals, you might consider volunteering at a local shelter. Maybe you love to write, so tutoring kids or adults in writing warms something up inside of you. Or if you love sports you could coach a local team."

Consider logistics. "If that opportunity to work in Africa at an AIDS clinic is screaming your name, consider how you are going to make that happen. You might ultimately end up there, but it might take some time. While you are waiting for things to fall into place, look in your own community at places you can serve until you're ready to board the plane. Make sure you have your ducks in a row, so to speak. I applied for my program in December, went through a discernment process in February, orientation in June and was on the plane in mid-July. This was extremely fast, most of the others in my program did not leave until August or September. While I was waiting, I stayed involved with things around my community and spent time with friends and family that I knew I would not see for a while."

Research your location. "If a particular location or line of volunteer work grabs at you, read more about it. Google it. Go to the library. Read about the language, culture, and history. Find blogs of people who live there currently, make connections with people and ask questions. Better yet, see if you can contact someone who is doing what you want to do and ask questions about it. The more you know the better off you are. You definitely don't want to commit any cultural faux pas in your host country, although they can be humorous and humbling."

Once you've made your way down that checklist, do as Chloe urged: "Go for it. Dive in. Jump in. Make that phone call, write that email, and submit your application."

She suggested looking into Peace Corps, The Amity Foundation, Humane Society, International Volunteer Programs Association, religious organizations, your local food bank or homeless shelter, community centers, Big Brothers Big Sisters, after school programs, and local women's shelters. In addition, international job fairs are a great place to make connections with recruiters abroad.

As Chloe said, "The right opportunity is out there, whether in your neighborhood or around the world. Take it!"

By traveling with their girlfriends, exploring places solo, and packing up to start over somewhere new, these divorcées embraced their second chances at life, answered their callings and changed the lives of others. Sometimes in order to find what you're really looking for, you just need to get out of town.

Eleven

Work it, Girl

A wife is basically a maid that pleases her husband at night. She should spend her days scrubbing floors (even if they were just washed the day before), fluffing bed pillows, and preparing meals for her provider. After a couple has a child, the wife should dedicate herself to family, discarding all of her own dreams and goals. This would all be true if we were living in the 1950s, but I've discovered that a shocking number of young marriages are ending because the male half of the partnership is still holding onto these ancient beliefs.

Modern day twenty-something women have the desire to meet only one of the ideals their 1950s counterparts brought to the forefront of society: their impeccable fashion sense. Declaring that a man will not hold them back from career-oriented goals, the only thing the following multi-tasking women served up were divorce papers. Here are just a few of the participants I spoke with who celebrated their divorces by focusing on their careers.

Miranda, 28, from Wisconsin, like The Getaway Girl, Casey, and myself, was unemployed while going through her divorce. To deal with it, Miranda, who married at 25, did the one thing that made her divorce struggles pale in comparison—she started her own business.

"I can honestly say I wouldn't change my decision for anything in the world," stated Miranda. "I have worked harder than I have in my entire life. I have buried myself in my work, sometimes to avoid reality and other times out of necessity."

Now, after almost a year of struggle, Miranda's divorce is nearly final and she is about to launch two blogging-related businesses.

Through her companies, Miranda is making a difference for fellow women. "Most of the traffic comes from college educated women, which makes me feel great considering I don't have a degree myself. I strongly believe that you can learn and advance without going to school if you don't have the means to go."

Launching her own businesses taught Miranda if she set her mind to something, she would achieve her goal. "I had no idea how to start a business, but I did. I started two. I also learned that you could surprise yourself. Even three years ago if you asked me if I thought I would be where I am today, I would have laughed and quite possibly said you were crazy."

For those thinking of taking a walk in Miranda's self-starting shoes, she suggests the following:

Find a team. "When you start a business, you simply cannot go it alone. It's just too much for one person. Utilize sites like PartnerUp, LinkedIn, and Twitter to find people who have an interest in what you want to do. The power of the Internet allows you to really work with anyone from anywhere. My team is located all over the United States."

Know that it's hard. "I won't sugar coat it. Think of it as having a fussy newborn plus a puppy and getting your doctorate all at once. Sometimes you won't know which way is up, what day it is, or be able to recall the last time you slept in your bed and not passed out at your desk."

Just do it. "If you really want it, you simply have to start. Form an LLC and get a website. Just start now and don't look back, don't second guess yourself. You will fail at some small battles, and you will get up, dust yourself off and begin again."

Miranda assured, "You will accomplish more than you ever thought you could and realize just how strong you really are. Knowing that is exactly what I needed. I am strong, I am capable and my companies helped me learn that more than any book, blog or kind words because I did it myself."

Since Rachel, 24, divorced, her life has gone to the dogs. The Maryland native, a life-long animal lover, who during times of turmoil often found solace in furry friends, married at age 20 and divorced after three years. This groomer clipped her then-husband because he lacked compassion towards animals. She's now dedicating her life to studying her true love: mammals.

Rachel's post-divorce goals include earning her Bachelor of Arts in biology and then going for her master's degree and possibly Ph.D. to work with wildlife.

Rachel shared, "My ex-husband was controlling and selfish. He enrolled himself in school and told me that once he was done then I could go. The only problem was that he failed every class. When I said, 'Since you've been flunking every class, I think I should go while you work,' he refused. So I kept working to support both of us."

Ending her marriage freed up a lot of money for Rachel, who is now enrolled in school full-time. "Through divorce, I got my life back. Instead of driving him around, replacing what he broke and paying for his living expenses, I now have that time and money to spend on myself."

Brooke from Wisconsin was married at 23 and divorced by age 27. "I was never supposed to get a divorce. I wasn't 'that girl.' Turns out, I am that girl, and now I love that I am that girl!," Brooke told me.

She stated, "I've realized my long-term goal of getting accepted into graduate school, quitting my job (that I didn't love, but also didn't truly hate), becoming a teaching assistant and working towards my master's, and eventually, my Ph.D. I've moved to a new city, as a result of school. I feel that, at the age of 28, my life is finally starting."

While some women used their divorces as an opportunity to further their careers, others opted to beef up their resumes with new skills.

Jackie, the 26-year-old scientist from Pennsylvania, taught herself a new language following her three-month marriage. "Learning a new language has helped me celebrate becoming a new person and looking forward to the possibility of a new, exciting life," Jackie told me. "I always wanted to have an extraordinary life—one that wasn't boring and about which I felt passionate."

Her new, fire-filled world began when Jackie started speaking German. "When referring to my ex, I usually use the word 'arsch,' which translates to 'ass.' Another good word to use is 'mistkerl,' which basically means 'douchebag.'"

When it comes to the rewards of divorce, women who are working it are reaping it, no matter what language they speak.

Twelve

Bling, Bling, Sell the Ring

After I got engaged, I'm pretty sure I stared at my ring so much that the glare of the diamonds became permanently embedded in my eyes, just like when someone takes a picture and the flash goes off in your face and then you're blind for a few minutes. I was that obsessed.

I even started to get my nails professionally done—something I never did before (and it has nothing to do with the fact that my childhood aspirations were to become a manicurist) to make sure my hands were always perfectly presentable. I took a million photos to get just the right angle so I could post online for everyone to see that I had achieved a very sparkly milestone. Like my shadow, my ring and I were inseparable. Until, of course, the day I stopped wearing it for good. That's when I learned that diamonds really are a girl's best friend. You see, once the relationship is over, you sell those diamonds and bask in the glow of something just as beautiful: cold hard cash.

Bling, bling, ladies, sell your ring and pamper yourself with the proceeds! Book a spa day, get the designer purse you've been eyeing, take a mini vacation, pay off debt, or put it in your child's college fund. Even more fun, buy a celebratory divorce ring, like 22-year-old Juniper from Oklahoma did when she divorced at age 20.

Juniper, who married when she was merely 18 years old, told me, "At the time of my engagement, a wedding ring symbolized hope and a happy future. By the end of my relationship it was more like a funeral shroud."

A series of jewelry advertisements inspired her to sell and splurge. Juniper described the ad jargon, saying, "The ads talked about how the left hand was a symbol of love, marriage, motherhood—the more co-dependent, nurturing side of a woman. They compared that to the right hand, which symbolized independence, empowerment, and loving yourself. I thought that was a beautiful idea. Leaving my left hand bare meant I was now a woman with no attachments or obligations to anyone. A diamond on that hand had once meant I was chained down and broken, but a fat rock on my right meant I was free and ruled my own world."

She purchased a sparkler for her middle finger. "It's a purple mystic topaz. In some light it looks violet, in others it's sort of bluish, and in others it has a definite green cast. The band is platinum and there are intricate floral accents around the main stone, with tiny diamonds set around," detailed Juniper.

Not everyone finds it so easy to part with her ring, however. Belle from Indiana is one of those women. Rather than sell her ring, Belle put it to eternal rest by purchasing a wedding ring coffin after her husband walked out on her.

Belle, who got married on Halloween, explained, "I was browsing online and found the ring that I guess is considered my divorce ring. I felt so odd taking off my wedding set."

"I've been keeping in mind my daughter may want to see them someday, so I'm keeping the rings. All I've done is think of her," stated Belle.

She'll be using the coffin as a prop for her "trash the dress" photo shoot, during which Belle will pose as a 1950s widow. "I'll be pretending to pour gasoline around the gas station where my ex met the woman he now lives with, and basically went to when he walked out," said Belle of her upcoming shoot.

Speaking of trash the dress photo shoots...

Thirteen

Trash the Dress

I trashed my wedding dress to celebrate my divorce, but dress trashing actually originated with newlyweds! Let me explain.

"Trash the dress" is a style of post-wedding photography. Typically, newlyweds re-create their elegant wedding day look and pose for photos in a contrasting environment. For example, a husband and wife may choose to "trash the dress" during a beach photo shoot by rolling around in the sand and running into the ocean. Or, the couple may opt to throw cupcakes on each other, or splatter one another with paint. Think cute, romantic and colorful.

As young divorcées, we're taking the art of wedding dress destruction to a whole other level by trashing the dress and everything it represents. We're metamorphosing an ugly and often shameful social status into a beautiful, celebratory moment. And, we're giving our mothers a reason to take down those photos of us as brides that still loom on the living room walls!

By doing "trash the dress" divorce photo shoots, we are leading an empowering movement that declares commitment only to our brand new selves.

Not only do "trash the dress" divorce photo shoots provide an outlet to unleash pent up anger, but also an opportunity to get pampered with professional hair and makeup services. After your physical and emotional transformation is complete, you'll feel way hotter than you ever did when you were married. The resulting photos will be your sweet revenge.

Fiona from Maryland knows firsthand. The former beach bride appropriately trashed her low-cut, sheer, flowy dress in the ocean. "It was my absolute dream beach wedding dress. I had it picked out long before I had even met my future ex-husband," admitted Fiona.

She told me, "I debated for a very long time about what to do with my dress. I had paid $300 to preserve it—almost as much as the dress cost—so originally I was going to sell it."

While her son was on his first vacation with his father, Fiona decided a photo shoot would be the perfect way to stay busy. So she took a day trip and made some waves of her own, as an audience gathered to watch.

"The photographer kept telling me to look angry and I told him I wasn't angry at the dress, just at my ex! The dress reminded me of my perfect wedding day, but really I didn't feel much. It was fun and sexy!"

She continued, "I was going to rip the dress, but decided that after I would donate it a cancer website."

Fiona doesn't regret parting with her dream dress. "I think they are beautiful shots and honestly what does anyone ever do with an old wedding dress anyway? I have a son, but even if I had a daughter, in 25 years she wouldn't want my dress," she concluded.

Vera, a 28-year-old butcher from Australia, slaughtered her dress. Calling her gown "a cheap version of what I really wanted," Vera custom designed on a tight budget. There was no sweet sorrow in this parting.

Describing her photo session, Vera told me, "I ripped it apart just like he did to my heart. Then, I spray-painted it black and pink, as my ex was a trade spray-painter and I thought it was appropriate! I then rubbed grease from my car on it, as my dream dress was sacrificed because my ex bought a car that cut into my wedding budget. Finally, I burned it, along with a photo of my ex and I from our honeymoon. I wanted it to be gone out of my life once and for all!"

Vera savored every moment as she created a beautiful disaster. "I loved ripping it apart giving it a new look with the paint, but the best part was seeing that sucker go up in flames! It was as if a huge weight had been lifted off my shoulders. The dress was no longer left hanging in the wardrobe; it was in a pile of ashes with me having the biggest smile I've smiled in a long, long time. It was the most exhilarating feeling, as I made it fun. It wasn't about him, it was all about me moving forward in my life and having fun getting there!"

Though she received negative feedback from some family and friends, Vera affirmed, "I have not one regret. Those comments aren't worth my time, I did it for me and not them!" She also noted, "I've had some real positives come out of it, too. It's inspired me to do more photo shoots with some lovely ladies in my life, who need a boost like this has done for me."

Caroline, 24 from Pennsylvania, said, "Trashing my dress was the most liberating, empowering feeling in the world."

Of the moment, she told me, "There I stood, in my perfectly clean wedding dress, with my veil on thinking to myself, 'I really hate this dress.' When my photographer said, 'Sit down in the meadow and look pissed off,' I looked at her and said, 'I'm happily divorced, how do I look pissed off?' She responded with, 'Think of your ex.' That line alone made my face goes sour."

Caroline's "trash the dress" shoot started in a meadow with her dressed as a visionary bride, including bunches of flowers in her hair and wedding rings on her finger. Slowly, her bored expressions turned to smiles, as she threw off her veil, let her up-do loose and moved the shoot to the back of a dump truck. After that, things got really dirty.

"I took a deep breath and walked right into a huge mud puddle," said Caroline. "The water was murky and my dress started to disappear. I then picked up slimy globs of mud and threw it down on my white, beaded dress. I proceeded to rip it, put sticks through it, and stubbed a cigarette butt out on it."

She hated her dress to begin with, citing, "This was the first dress my mom picked out, and the first and only dress I tried on. She fell in love with it, and would not let me try on any other dresses. I didn't have any say in this because she was paying. I then had to get straps added to it, which I did not want either. I was miserable and very glad to get rid of that thing."

Now, she announced, "I'm finally laughing, and smiling at everything."

Ready to get glam and forget about the ball and chain for good? Here are some divorcée "trash the dress" style photo shoot ideas:

Light it on fire—at your own risk. *Be sure to take all precautionary measures on this one.* "If I had thought about this before I had thrown my dress in the trash, I would've kept the dress for my divorce party. I would've had it on display with sharpies for all my guests to write my ex-husband a message, or write me a blessing, or whatever they felt like writing to celebrate my divorce. Then, I would've built a fire and set the dress ablaze," sighed Mae from Massachusetts.

Graffiti with your girls. Have your former bridesmaids spray paint words of encouragement on the dress as you wear it.

Reconstruct your gown. Cut it into a mini dress or chop off the corset and turn it into a sexy night on the town top! "I'll change it into a wild mini-skirt, crazy party dress!" exclaimed Monica from Hong Kong.

Get crafty. Dye your dress a vibrant color. Then cover it in glitter. "I would shorten it to my knees to make it a super cute, flowing number. I would dye it a bright color, orange or blue maybe. Then

I would get an amazing pair of shoes to go with it," fantasized Lily from Virginia.

Wax poetic. Write lyrics from your favorite break-up song all over the dress.

Go vintage. Put on pin-up girl clothing, rent a vintage car and then drive over your dress.

Smock-it-up. Wear it while you paint the walls of your new or improved home.

Paws for a good time. Love dogs? Frolic in the dog park and let your four-legged friends cover you in kisses and mud.

Go Wild West. Grab your cowboy boots and go horseback riding. "I would go horseback riding through some mud puddles with it on," said Rory from Massachusetts. "I've never been horseback riding before and it is on my bucket list. Also, it is something my ex-husband never would have done with me."

Stop whining and make some wine! Go grape stomping in your gown. Everyone looks good in purple.

Ink it. Have your favorite tattoo artist create a mural on your dress. After your shoot, auction it for charity.

Turn it into an art project for your kids. Divorced with children? Hand your kids finger paints and let them go crazy. This is also a fun way to show them that divorce is not necessarily a bad thing.

Jump in a mosh pit. This one is for the music lovers. Just be careful if you're stage diving at festivals. Those crowds are rowdy!

Make it a family event. "All of my friends and family would each get a pair of scissors and help me cut it up. I would save the neckline with the beautiful beading, though. Maybe use it in something else," pondered Chloe from Texas.

Make throw pillows! Love to sew? Cut up the fabric, dye it, and add cute buttons. Or, make a brand new dress like Cherie from California suggested: "I want to have all my closest friends find some ridiculously cheesy wedding dresses from thrift stores and pick their favorite part of the dress and take it off. Then I want to sew those parts onto my dress."

Host an art therapy party. Invite friends over, cut the dress into squares and have everyone paint one. Then, frame each square and hang on your walls.

Suit up. Turn your dress into a bikini! Justine from New York says she'd enjoy "trashing it on a beautiful beach to symbolize that beach wedding I didn't get!"

Make your own freedom flag. Cut it up, sew on patterns, paint phrases. Make it represent you!

Participate in a color run. You'll have a rainbow revamp of your gown after the marathon.

Look hot. If your wedding dress doesn't fit anymore, don't fret! Buy a sexy new dress and wear it as you destroy your gown.

Get revenge. Pick a setting or theme that reminds you of your ex-husband and incorporate that into your shoot.

Get on track. "I would make it into a track outfit and run my first half marathon in it," imagined Hadley from New York.

If you choose to trash your dress, remember to put safety first. Take all precautions when partaking in photo shoots near water. Do not attempt to pose near raging water or in large, deep bodies of water. Remember, wedding gowns are even heavier when wet and will drag you down. The above suggestions are meant to spark creativity, but each situation is unique. Make sure you are in a harmless setting.

One last reminder: Trash your dress at your own risk. The point of these photo shoots is to celebrate the end of your marriage, not to prove you're a daredevil. Though, I'm sure you can be a bit risqué in the right situation!

Fourteen

Get a Divorce Tattoo

It's time to touch on an often-painful topic: tattoos. There are two reasons a woman gets a divorce tattoo, either to cover up body art she got in honor of her marriage, or to commemorate her fabulous, post-divorce life. I'm still pondering what to do about my "XO," but Lily from Virginia sure knew how to obscure her newlywed inspired ink.

She filled me in, "The original tattoo was the first letter of my married last name. It was a smaller version of the same tattoo my husband had on his back. I had actually originally hated it on him, and he used to joke that he would make me get the same one if we ever got married. But over the years we were together it somehow became serious, so a few weeks after our wedding I was at the tattoo shop. I felt so proud of it at first. I would show it off to everyone, and it seemed like such a special way to always feel joined with him, even when we weren't together."

When the pair split, Lily viewed the tattoo as a constant reminder of sadness and anger. "I was almost obsessed with the idea of covering it up, but knew I needed to wait until I had an idea that would be meaningful, and that I wouldn't associate with the tattoo underneath."

She decided on an image of the Brooklyn Bridge and Manhattan skyline. "New York is where I moved after college, and it was a crucial step in my personal development. My husband and I eventually left the city, but I moved back after we broke up, and this time it helped me develop into my new single self," revealed Lily. "The city was there for me in a way that my ex never was, and it seemed perfect that I cover up a reminder of him with something that not only helped me to heal, but that I will love forever, unlike him."

Lily considered her divorce tattoo "a reminder of my strength and how proud I am that I'm constantly working on being the best version of myself."

Pearl, a 26-year-old preschool teacher from Tennessee, also redesigned her dedicational body art. She originally inked a daisy with a stem in the shape of the letter "J," the first initial of her then-husband's name, on her forearm. "It now says 'Just breathe,' as a constant reminder that everything will be OK, that I should slow down and breathe," Pearl told me.

While married, Bethany from Ohio etched her husband's name on her ankle along with a meaningful phrase. "He got the same on his forearm, with my name," she noted.

Bethany first attempted to get her tattoo removed, however her dermatologist advised that it most likely would not completely fade because of her skin tone. Now, her plan is to cover it with the image of a moth, inspired by a quote from a domestic abuse survival book.

While Bethany plans to commemorate escaping her abuser, Juniper from Oklahoma told me about getting tattooed to celebrate the end of a controlling marriage. Of her ex-husband, Juniper said, "I always wanted to get tattooed but he hated them and told me under no circumstances would he allow me to have one. As soon as I filed for divorce, three friends and I drove to Joplin, Missouri so I could get the tattoo of my dreams."

The design, located on her left shoulder blade, is based on an antique lock. "It's heart-shaped with an intricate floral engraving," described Juniper. She continued, "A chain sweeps from the lock across my back to my spine where a skeleton key dangles. It symbolizes the importance of guarding your heart. I should have been more careful with mine. From now on, I keep my heart locked up because it's precious, and I have the only key. Someday I hope someone will have the matching key, but right now it's just me."

Chloe from Texas memorializes periods of her life through tattoos, so it was only natural to add a divorce-related work of art. The lower right side of her back is decorated with images of a phoenix and the Chinese symbol for double happiness. "Both are very traditional symbols of love—something I haven't given up on in my life," affirmed Chloe. "The phoenix represents my renewed life, a life of joy and purpose rising from the ashes of the old one. The double-happiness symbol comes from a Chinese tale about lovers who find each other—they each draw half of the symbol. I'm not giving up on finding someone to double my happiness! I got this tattoo during a year-long mission in China, a year that helped me catch my breath between the end of my marriage and the next phase of my life. It's about moving on with a positive attitude towards what is next in my life."

Sounds like Chloe and Pearl have something in common! Ariel from New Jersey also got fresh ink for her fresh start. However, a dog inspired Ariel's. No, not her ex-husband—a real dog! The beagle she rescued from a shelter after her divorce.

Ariel explained, "I grew up with dogs all my life. My ex and I had adopted a cat, and then once we moved into our house, I figured I would throw around the idea of adopting a dog. He said I would ignore the cat and have one more thing to take care of—how nice."

Around the time of her divorce proceedings, Ariel figured it was the perfect opportunity. "I felt like adopting my dog helped me step out of the life I had before by starting over fresh. She was getting a new life with me and I was starting my new 'free' life over with her. She has been the best choice (after divorcing) that I have made and she brings me happiness."

That's where the tattoo comes into play. Ariel enthused, "I even got a pink paw print tattoo for her and our new start!"

Adding to her collection, Ariel later went under the needle to get the letter "A" with a crown on it. "It's a sign of me being the 'queen' or 'princess' of my life. I control what I do and no one else."

Taking the reigns, Ariel's first order of business was to throw herself a divorce party, and it turns out she's not the only one.

Fifteen

Host a Divorce Party

Divorce parties are the new weddings. Between novelties and greeting cards, divorce rituals have become so much fun that even single and happily married people are envious of newly crowned divorcettes.

As previously stated, Ariel from New Jersey's first order of post-divorce business was to throw a celebratory event, complete with a "free at last" banner she constructed herself from a "happy birthday" banner. And she made a matching cake. Take that, Martha Stewart.

Joined by close friends in her home, Ariel set her past up in flames. "I found a picture of my ex-husband and I from our wedding, tore it in half so that it was just my ex, then I tore my ex into pieces. My friends and I each took one and went outside and burned them with a lighter," said Ariel.

"The divorce party really helped to close part of my past out, and it sounds so odd, but burning the picture was like a huge piece to moving on. Watching the picture turn to ashes was like watching my new life start right then and there. I have loved every minute of the post-divorce life I have started."

Rory from Massachusetts also showered herself with a divorce party. She even had a theme: "Good-bye abhorrence, hello passion!"

Detailing her adult-toy themed party, Rory confided, "In my marriage, I was the sexually unfulfilled partner and I yearned for real intimacy constantly. Celebrating my own sexuality and unabashed desires as a woman by taking matters into my own hands, literally, has been a very big part of my recovery process."

Guests noshed on mini chocolate penis-covered strawberries while Rory toasted to her new life and new man! "The celebration reminded me that I am truly loved by many and it also reminded me how grateful I am to have support in my decision to leave my marriage after only two years."

Belle from Indiana hit a piñata and then painted the town red, or shall I say pink. It turns out hot pink limos *do* exist and Belle and her pals were escorted in one!

Samantha, 28, from Pennsylvania opted to live it up during a long weekend in Las Vegas. While flipping through a travel magazine, Samantha said, "I came upon an article that talked about how there were a few clubs in Vegas that not only specialized in bachelorette parties, but also hosted divorce parties. I had never heard of that concept. I mean, who celebrates a divorce? But after mourning the failure of my marriage for months, I was finally reaching the stage of acceptance and beginning to embrace my new status of being single. I brought up the topic of the article to my friends and they loved the idea! We made the trip all about friendship, with minimal talk about men."

Samantha recalled, "Having my best friends there to share that feeling with me and support me was beyond words. They supported me through the entire ordeal. Once I told them that my ex and I were getting a divorce, I went from being embarrassed and feeling like a failure, to feeling like I had an army behind me. And having them support me in the idea of a divorce party solidified it all for me."

Molly from Massachusetts celebrates her annual divorceiversary. "My divorce was official on Cinco de Mayo, so every year I have a reason to go out with friends and toast to my wonderful single life," said Molly. "I celebrate because it is a way to remind myself to be proud of who I am and that I was strong enough to make it through a really horrible thing. I don't ever want to be ashamed of it again."

One thing is for sure; no one in this book blushes anymore when faced with the subject of divorce. And it's never too late to celebrate. Samantha has one tip for those who are divorce party planning and that is "Make sure the day is all about you."

Here are some of her suggestions:

- Indulge in spa treatments.
- Grab drinks and have dinner at your favorite restaurant.
- Take a weekend ski trip.
- Do a weekend winery tour.
- Host a makeup party or wine and cheese party at your new 'single' apartment.

Samantha urged, "Do something for you. Celebrate the survivor within. You will get through this. And you will be a better you for having gone through it."

Sixteen

Start Something

When your life is falling apart, it's easy to host a self-pity party in your bedroom. However, sobbing won't get you anywhere—except maybe the drug store to buy another box of tissues. Face it; the universe gave you a big sour lemon when it brought along your ex-husband. Now, break out the little plastic umbrellas and stir up some lemonade. You've got a revolution to start.

Your divorce happened for a reason. Figure out what that reason was, the lesson it brought, and what you can do to influence the lives of others based on your knowledge. Start something. Whether it is a *Trash the Dress* support group in your area (hint, hint, contact me!) or a meet-up for single moms, now is the time to go full speed ahead. Impacting others will change your own world in the process.

Ana from the Philippines (remember, there is no legal divorce in her country) told me that after she had removed the negative people from her life and paid off her debt, she reached a point where she had ticked off everything on her post-divorce checklist. Then, she started a career as a journalist. "I realized that I was in a position to change the stigma and stereotype about solo moms," said Ana. "It makes it easier to do things beyond yourself when your basics are covered."

Ana chronicled the early years of her limbo status on a blog. Through her work, she said, "I've found that resources for women undergoing annulment or something similar are scarce. So I published my own book-journal, *Happy Even After: A Solo Mom's Journal.*

Ana, who is now 37, realized she needed another outlet to devote her energies after her daughter reached adulthood. "That was the start of how I got involved in advocacy work for solo moms, women's sexual health rights in the Philippines, and HIV/AIDS awareness," she told me.

Back in America, fellow single mom, Fiona, also took action. After her divorce, Fiona began running and signed up for a half marathon. Inspired by the event, Fiona announced, "I founded a 5k race to raise money to support a local domestic violence shelter." The race generates revenue for a longstanding community service provider helping residents who have been impacted by domestic violence, sexual assault, and child abuse. Thanks to Fiona, a dark situation is brought to light and she was pleased to report the whopping $10,451.50 raised by her first annual event.

Domestic violence awareness is a cause close to the heart of Bethany from Ohio, as she's a survivor who once had to seek refuge in a women's shelter. Bethany swears if she stayed married, she'd be "dead or in prison. Dead if he accidentally killed me; in prison if I retaliated and killed him."

Bethany suggested divorced women donate their gowns to an organization called The Wedding Dress Project. "They accept dress donations and use them in dress deconstruction workshops where participants deconstruct and reconstruct the dress. The purpose is to help victims of domestic violence cope and move past their experiences," explained Bethany.

She continued, "I still believe in love and the beauty that marriage can be. So my wedding dress donation would be for someone who may not have money to buy an expensive dress but would like to marry the man of her dreams. Maybe a bad dress experience for me could be the good dress a woman has always dreamed of."

That would certainly start something beautiful.

Seventeen

Own Your Status

Our marital status does not define us, unless we let it. Seriously, who wants to be referred to as somebody's divorced friend, when they can be introduced as an *American Idol*-worthy singer or "the funniest person you'll ever meet?" Once you own your status, even if the "D" word comes up in conversation, you'll have it covered.

Nora, the family attorney from North Carolina, encouraged all young divorcées to take pride in their status. "Know what happened in your divorce and be honest about how the experience changed and shaped you," advised Nora.

She shared eight steps for rocking the divorcée title:

1. **Remember the positive.** "It can be hard to remember that there are actually some upsides to divorce. When you own your divorced status, you get to own those benefits. What are the benefits? Knowledge of what it really feels like to be married, more realistic relationship expectations, independence, the ability to work through difficult times, and a stronger sense of yourself."

2. **Don't hide.** "Whether you want to hold the divorcée label or not, you are divorced. You're going to feel more genuine and intact if you embrace being divorced rather than trying to hide it. There is a temptation to try to forget your past marriage and divorce and not to share the experience with others, but the truth is that it happened and it's OK. It's really empowering to say, 'Yeah, I was married and divorced and it was difficult, but I'm doing great now.'"

3. **Redefine the "divorced" term.** "Help change the stigma associated with being divorced. We all know that divorce has its benefits and that there are tons of fabulous divorcées! The more you embrace your past with confidence and are open about your experience, the more positive associations with divorce we can put into the world."

4. **Change the narrative**. "It is scary, at first, to own your divorcée identity to the world. There is fear of judgment and alienation. Once you get past this initial fear, however, you'll feel free and that fear will no longer have power over you. When I was first divorced and people (distant friends or even our shared doctors) would ask how my husband was doing, I would shrug and say 'fine' and quickly squirm away. I would have avoided that specific question, but I still felt the shame and apprehension associated with being dishonest. Now, I calmly tell anyone who asks that I think he is doing well (Note: Nora even attended his second wedding!). People are often taken aback, sometimes sympathetic, and sometimes pry for more information. Because I am not ashamed of the experience, I can handle all reactions and no longer fear the questioning. It's unbelievably freeing."

5. **Connect through divorce.** "You will very likely find kinship and support and maybe even a next mate in other divorcées. If you don't speak your story out loud, you can miss the opportunity to meet other divorcées, or to hear inspiring and comforting stories of divorces that end happily."

6. **Know you're not alone.** "As a divorce lawyer, I can tell you from lots of experience that there are plenty of people who are divorced and don't admit to it or talk about it. When I share with my clients that I am divorced, they feel more comfortable sharing their stories. When I talk about being a divorce lawyer, others open up with their own stories of divorce in their own life or in their family. More than half of the adult population has been divorced and more than that have been affected by it."

7. **Don't rush it.** "Probably the most common statements I hear from recent divorcées is that they want to 'move on' and 'put it behind' them. I hear you. I wanted that immediately, too. The thing is, to really move on from being divorced you have to really own the experience, make some sense of it, and incorporate it into who you are going to be. Divorce won't un-happen by denying it."

8. **Create your own label.** "When you are at peace with being a divorcée, you get to create the narrative that goes with that title. Society has its own story that goes along with divorce, and chances are it doesn't fit your unique situation. I'm sure you have a 'party line' about what happened in your marriage and divorce. Acceptance will allow you to attach the truth to your divorcée identity instead of generic assumptions about a marriage gone awry. Or worse, rumors and speculation!"

Of course, owning your status, as Nora suggests, may take some time. Working with the experience of her divorce, not against it, was Nora's secret. Sure, people may whisper behind your back about your past marriage, but by owning your status, you turn those words of failure into jealousy.

Eighteen

Go Outside Your Comfort Zone

I got naked in a room full of about 30 strangers, who also just so happened to be in their birthday suits, and a camera crew captured every moment.

After I left Max, I gained a renewed sense of freedom and excitement for life. So when my friend Adam asked me to be an extra in a music video for his band, I figured it was as good a time as any to celebrate the new Joelle.

It didn't even matter that I had the worst haircut of my life the day we filmed. I had the weight of the world literally off my shoulders. Wearing nothing but flesh colored panties and electrical tape across my boobs, I was at my most vulnerable, yet felt strong and confident. Such risky behavior put me outside of my comfort zone, but I'm glad I pushed myself to go there. Hey, some people wear less to the beach! Bottom line: I never would have done this when I was married.

I'm not the only one who did something she'd never imagine. Harper from Arizona found her voice—and second husband— when she pushed aside her insecurities and fears of rejection and picked up a karaoke microphone.

She told me, "I had never sung in front of others before, despite all my friends telling me I should. At one point after my divorce, while looking for work, I saw an ad online for a local karaoke host position. Long story short, I got the job, and was responsible for hosting a show."

She described one night in particular, "About an hour before closing, a group of guys arrived, and walked right past me to sit at the bar. One of them made eye contact with me. I remember loving his blue eyes and dark hair—my weakness! Later, as I was singing a song about dancing, I felt someone behind me. I turn around, and there was Blue Eyes, dancing all up on me, obviously not completely sober. I thought he was funny and harmless, so I politely pushed him away and kept singing."

Eight months later, Harper and Blue Eyes moved in together. Soon after, they learned she was pregnant. "We added our beautiful baby girl to our family that already included three boys—my son, and his two sons," happily reported Harper, who now has a dancing partner for life.

Cherie from California actually credits dancing as her savior. "I do not give a crap if I suck at dancing. It saved me," she told me.

Cherie elaborated, "Dancing brought me back to happiness in a way that nothing else did after my divorce. I realized that dancing is not just an action, it's a feeling, and those feelings can set you free."

She began dancing in the privacy of her home. As she explained, Cherie rewound to the days following her divorce: "I started by playing all these awful break-up songs, just sitting there crying like a moron. Then I thought, 'What the hell is my problem?' There are some pretty 'effed up break-up songs out there. They were actually making me even more depressed! So, I started listening to the cheesiest songs about surviving breakups. And I danced. I don't mean like choreographed, professional dancing. I mean ridiculous moves that shouldn't be allowed in public."

But then, she brought her skills into society. "When I realized what it was doing to my body and mind, I started looking for every possible way to dance. Those moments of joy I felt when I danced started to transcend into my everyday life. It started to effect everything and got to the point where I was able to start feeling that joy even when I was not dancing. This was so foreign to me. I had not felt this joy, with the exception of a few fleeting moments, in over six years. It was at the point where my friends and family started to notice that I was over-flowing with happiness."

Cherie concluded, "Dance saved me because it allowed me to be transported out of my body and brought to this alternate world. This crazy, beautiful, serene world that did not even entertain all the bullshit I was dealing with in my life. For those moments I was so happy and free. I felt beautiful and confident. Everything I forgot about myself over the years I was married started to creep back into my mind."

She urged her peers to follow her lead. "It does not have to be a certain type of music. It can be anything from jazz to rap to house music. That's the beauty of dance; you can dance slow, fast, jump around, wave your arms, stomp your feet, or wiggle your ass. It doesn't matter how you move your body, as long as you *feel*."

We all have something that we just refuse to do because it makes us feel insecure, whether it's wearing a bikini, dancing, singing, or doing standup. Let these stories inspire you to step outside your comfort zone and conquer your reservations. You just may end up booking up your social life...and meeting your soul mate!

Nineteen

Throw Out the Rulebook

Society's standards forced marriage upon many of us, whether imposed by religion, parents or ourselves. We've lived and learned that those rules are a bunch of crap. If anything, following tradition sometimes leads you on a miserable path. Luckily, we've got a chance to get our lives back on track. Many of us have thrown out the rulebook and begun to write our own.

Maureen, a 29-year-old attorney from Oregon told me, "I felt like my whole life, I was told a lot of rules that led me down the path to divorce. For me, the divorce process has been about making my own rules."

Here's what Maureen learned from following the rules:

"Rule" 1—If you're dating a guy for more than a year, he should be putting a ring on it. "There is no such thing as a five year plan. If you're agreeing to spend eternity with someone, there's nothing shameful about being sure. Especially today when women are having children well into their late 30s, there is no reason to rush into marriage. Relationships aren't a video game. You don't have to always be thinking about getting to the next level. Just enjoy the moment you're in.'"

"Rule" 2—Don't live with a guy before you get married. "I was raised in a strict Catholic family. Even though my mom knew I was not a virgin, she would not have been OK with me living with him before marriage. She convinced us you had to 'save that magic' for marriage. You don't truly know someone until you live with them. Daily habits are what's most important, not how he makes you feel a few date nights a week."

"Rule" 3—Marry a guy who is crazier about you than you are about him. "Probably the saddest thing my mom ever taught me. But I followed it. I had my heart broken before and this time, I married him because I knew he'd never leave me. I know now that I want someone who I am crazy about—and if I'm afraid of him leaving me, that's a good thing. It will keep me on my toes. The best relationships are when both people stay on their toes like that."

"Rule" 4—Don't date divorcées. Especially not divorced dads with kids. "You know their damage and most of the time it's the same as yours. Even better, they know the mistakes they made the first time and aren't interested in repeating them. And as for kids? Just keep an open mind. I never thought I was a kid person but now I'm really enjoying the dimension my boyfriend's kids add to my life. It's like going shopping. If you say, 'I'm only going to look at green shirts,' you'll miss the red one that you might have ended up loving."

"Rule" 5—Sex is not the most important thing in a relationship. "It is such a myth that marriage is just the end of sex and women should moan and groan and fake a headache to get out of it. Sex bonds a couple. Sex is what distinguishes a friendship from a relationship. If there isn't any sex in your marriage, congrats, you have a roommate. Don't be ashamed of being a human with a sex drive. And don't be ashamed if your spouse isn't doing it for you. You can't choose to whom you are attracted."

"Rule" 6—Marriage is supposed to be hard. "It's true that marriage isn't always going to be easy. But the good should outweigh the bad. The people who say otherwise are just stuck in their own miserable marriages."

"Rule" 7—You have to try counseling before throwing in the towel. "My ex-husband and all my friends judged me because I was unwilling to try counseling. But I am a decisive person and I knew that I wasn't committed to making it work. I still feel confident that it was the right thing not to give my ex false hope. I saw my mom torture herself for years with the list of gripes my dad had come up with when they were in counseling after they ultimately got divorced. If it's not working, it's not working. No need to beat a dead horse."

"Rule" 8—Cheating is the cause of divorce. "After I left, my ex went on an inquisition to figure out if I'd been cheating—talking to all my friends, even my sister, and hacking into my phone records online. To him, it couldn't possibly be about anything other than our marriage being broken. Even in relationships where there was infidelity, that wasn't the cause of the break-up. Chances are, things were bad way before that."

"Rule" 9—You can't meet good men at bars. "OK, that one might be true. I met my ex-husband at a bar."

"Rule" 10—Chicks before dicks. "Girlfriends are fickle. Don't count on them to be there when you leave, especially if their spouses/boyfriends are friends with your ex. They will most likely side with their spouse/boyfriend to protect their own relationship."

"Rule" 11—Divorce = failure. "Again, the people who say this are the ones who are stuck and don't have the balls to leave. Divorce just means the relationship ran its course and you don't want to live the rest of your life miserably."

"Rule" 12—Rain on your wedding day is good luck. "At least it was not in my case."

"Rule" 13—Opposites attract. "It's OK to be different from your spouse but common core beliefs and shared interests keep you together for the long haul. My ex and I were just too different and we ended up leading separate lives."

"Rule" 14—Keeping your finances separate will create space between you. "There's nothing unhealthy about each person having 'carte blanche' with some money. Too many fights start because one person's spending priorities don't align with the other's."

"Rule" 15—You should change your last name. "Just remember what a pain it is going to be to change it back if you're in the 50 percent who don't make it."

"Rule" 16—You'll be OK as long as he can make you laugh. "Telling knock-knock jokes won't keep the fire going into the bedroom."

"Rule" 17— Divorce is just too complicated. It's easier to stay. "When I first started thinking about leaving, I was talking to a friend about it and said stuff like, 'But we can't sell the house in this market' and 'Who would get the dogs?' She gave me the best advice that I kept thinking back to until I was ready. She said 'There will come a time when none of that matters. And then you know you have to leave.' It was true."

"Rule" 18—All people are basically good. "Wrong. All people are basically selfish so you'd better look out for yourself. My most popular mantra after the divorce became, 'What you think about me is none of my business,' because people are crappy and they judge. Bottom line, you have to ask yourself, 'Do I believe this person has my best interest at heart?' And if you can't say 'yes,' then you shouldn't have them in your life, even if it's only your perception. People are going to be crappy to you after you leave, especially mutual friends. Remember, you are changing their world and change makes people uncomfortable. You will be disappointed and surprised by their actions but all you can do is look out for yourself. That's what they're all doing anyway."

"Rule" 19—You are going to be really depressed when you're going through divorce. "I certainly had times of sadness but for the most part, I was excited to finally be moving on. My mom, who was left by my dad after 25 years of marriage, made me feel like I should be sad all the time like she had been. I had to accept that even though that had been her experience, it was OK that it wasn't mine."

"Rule" 20—You should stay single for a while after you divorce to 'find yourself.' "This was my biggest struggle after I left. Everybody kept telling me that you have to 'find yourself' and 'be alone' before coupling up again. Finally, I realized that I had found myself a long time ago. That was why I had left. Now I was ready to be with someone I wanted to be with. People weren't meant to be alone. And that's OK."

To sum up Maureen's list, there's one rule you should be sure you follow: Break all the rules.

Twenty

Give Yourself a New Last Name

I always hated my last name. No one ever pronounced it correctly and in elementary school, some kids even jokingly called me Joelle Computer. Ouch. I could not wait to change my last name after marriage. Sure, the government processes are annoying, but I felt like a new person, someone who had conquered her past and didn't cringe every time she picked up a prescription at the pharmacy.

Then, I got divorced and wanted to snarl at every telemarketer or person who called me by my married last name. I dragged my feet when it came to the hassle of changing over my credit card information post-divorce and it came back to bite me. On one vacation, Frank and I were checking into the hotel and since I made the reservations, I had to show the guest services coordinator my credit card. My old name was still on it and the guy actually called us Mr. and Mrs. "insert married last name here." Talk about awkward! Just what I needed to happen on our first getaway. Thankfully, Frank just ignored it.

Now the only last name annoyances I deal with are when I'm logging into my bank account online and have to answer the security question, "Where did you meet your spouse?" I think it's time I change banks.

I'm sure many of you can relate. But one divorcée who definitely doesn't have to deal with these scenarios is Marion, a 29-year-old paralegal from Tennessee.

After two—yes, two—marriages and divorces during the second decade of her life, Marion not only created her own label, she gave herself a new last name. By new last name, I don't mean Marion legally went back to her maiden name. She created a brand new identity.

"When I was getting divorced, I never really thought much about going back to my maiden name," Marion told me. "I felt like I had already lived that life and needed a fresh start. This new life needed a new last name. One that made me feel as bold, strong and free as the divorce did."

Marion chose to use her unique middle name as her last name. "I had heard the story about my middle name my whole life and it was so intriguing. Enchanting, really. A story about a strong woman who was bold in times when patriarchy was the norm."

Advising those on the verge of changing their last names, Marion said, "I would suggest to anyone who is wanting to change their name, without the desire to go back to a maiden name, to look into their genealogy for a family name that they find intriguing or uplifting. They may also find that they like their mother's or grandmother's maiden name. I've had friends who've gone that route. And if that doesn't suit them, it may also be a good activity to try to look inside yourself and search for a word that most exemplifies how you feel after the divorce. And then use that to find a new last name. Like, hey, what's wrong with the last name 'Hope?'"

Twenty One

Discover Your Vow Factor

A s my spiritual healer, Ajnira, mentioned, we all lose a piece of ourselves while maintaining a long-term relationship. Though not intentional, it's natural. Those Saturday nights once spent bonding with besties soon become under-the-cover snugglefests during a movie and popcorn with your beau. Maybe your hobbies faded away during your marriage because you were so focused on building a lovenest. Now is the time to celebrate your reclaimed individuality and commit to enriching your life in every selfish way. Determine the talents that make you awesome and activities in which you excel and vow to focus on them.

Sara from Egypt reclaimed her right to rock. A musician since age six, Sara quit her band because of her then-husband. "My ex-husband told (not asked) me to leave the band because it was embarrassing and shameful to him and his family," Sara said.

Distressed, she sought her mother's opinion. "Her response after all these years she'd invested in my music was 'Honey, you are getting too old to be in a band.' I was heartbroken. But, I thought that to save my marriage this was what I needed to do. So I quit the band. And I felt more lost than ever."

Soon after, an opportunity arose and Sara secretly joined a new group of musicians. "Over four years, I tried to be as open, honest and forthcoming with my ex as I could possibly be despite the fact that I knew he was lying straight to my face about a lot of things, so I did something I'm not 100 percent proud of," she admitted. "I lied about practicing with a band. I would say I was going out—but would go jam instead. And it was worth it. Lying didn't fix my marriage. But the music is what really got me through and out of it. It was the only time I could be energetic."

Sara continued, "After my divorce, I kept with the band. It gave me that something to look forward to when the days were crawling by with no real goal in sight. We organized and played at a few clubs and got one of our songs professionally recorded. Now we're in the process of trying to get it on the radio here."

She concluded, "Music was my outlet. I wrote songs about what a horrible person my ex was to me, and how angry I was with people and society for trying to keep me in the marriage even when it was my ex who was at fault. On stage, I got to be the person I dreamt I was: confident and self-assured. And it was my celebration, that through this divorce, I got what I wanted and what I needed: my music, of which my ex tried to deny me, music that healed my soul."

Music was Sara's salvation. Maybe yours is painting. Or perhaps you're meant to be the next hot craft vendor online. You'll never know unless you vow to find and rock your "Wow."

Twenty Two

Begin a Bucket List

P laying it safe may have led you down the aisle. Now it's time to gamble on yourself. That's exactly what Hadley from New York did when she divorced at age 28.

"I've always been a free spirit, but played things safe for the most part, staying within my comfort zone. To hell with that! I'm going to gamble the right way. I'm all in, and hoping for a big win," said Hadley, pointing at the betting man she married.

To start, Hadley made a list of 101 things she wanted to do in 1,001 days. Some items she had never done before, others she wanted to revisit from her childhood. "It took me weeks to complete composing my list," Hadley told me. She continued, "Once it was done I published it online. The feedback I received from friends and family was overwhelming, a big self-esteem boost that I definitely needed after years of being in a relationship and marriage where I just felt sort of 'there.'"

Her loved ones jumped at the chance to be a part of her list, which included learning how to build a fire, and going kayaking, wakeboarding, and paddle boarding. "My 101 list is a mere starting point for me to take chances and try new things all while making memories and new friends along the way," Hadley stated.

Recent accomplishments include taking a hula hooping class, making her aunt's bolognese sauce recipe (Hadley was a vegetarian her entire marriage), changing a baby's diaper, eating filet mignon and sushi, enjoying a picnic, embarking on a haunted hayride, running on the beach, attending an Irish festival, and inspiring someone to create a 101 list of their own.

Risks, adventures and randomness Hadley plans to endure the next 1,001 days include:

Going on a hot air balloon ride. "I'm sort of a control freak, and I'm pretty sure they won't let me navigate the balloon, so I'll have to be medicated for sure."

Doing the Edgewalk at the CN Tower in Toronto. "I'm deathly afraid of heights. I may have a heart attack while living on the edge here, but that's what gambling is all about, taking chances. I've got a decent life insurance policy. My mom can buy herself a yacht should I drop dead in Toronto 1,168 feet above the ground."

Swimming with dolphins. "I'm afraid of fish in a pond so I'm a little skeptical of how I'm going to actually hold onto a large one."

Biking in the Tour de Cure. "I'm signed up to bike 40 miles and raise money for the American Diabetes Association with a group of my girlfriends."

Acting as chairperson and coordinator for the local Fashion Week 5K: "I have been chosen to coordinate a 5K race for my local Fashion Week which raises money for a local children's organization. I have never put together a race before, so this is both exciting and nerve-wracking. Runners are encouraged to dress up in things like tiaras, feather boas and old bridesmaid dresses."

Volunteering to help senior citizens: "I have volunteered with a local organization which grants wishes to seniors in area nursing homes. I find charity work to be so rewarding and since my divorce have a newfound appreciation for it."

When her list is complete, Hadley assured, "I'll create a new one. I have OCD, lists are my best friend." She advised others, "I don't believe anything in life is about how fast you finish. Do things at your own speed, and take it all in along the way. There will be bumps in the road, but that's what spices things up."

Grace from Pennsylvania is also embarking on a "things I've always wanted to do list," post-divorce. She told me her divorce was simultaneously tragic and liberating. "At 28 I was finally free to do what every 22-year-old should: individuate and spread my wings, get to know me and to become happy and secure with that me. I have seized by the horns the opportunity to individuate."

Describing her list, Grace said, "After my divorce I adopted a dog. I love dogs and had always wanted one, but my ex had always said it was 'not the right time' to get one (not to delve into realms of psychotherapy, but my parents had given me the same line growing up). So I made the decision to get a dog. I commented to my therapist that I was not sure why this felt like such a big deal to me. She responded that of course it was a big deal—I had actually made a decision for myself. Not bound by what my parents thought, or what my ex thought, I decided to get a dog."

She also started trying new recipes, hosting holidays, and backpacked around Europe for a month. As for what's next, Grace informed me, "I plan to build a headboard for my bed and I have been learning about antiquing techniques to refinish some old furniture. I have been composting and plan to start a vegetable garden. I am doing my own taxes for the first time ever this year. I am learning about and developing my appreciation for indie films and music. Out of context, these activities are mundane. But their importance lies in the fact that they are mine, and no one else's. And in the end, I must be a whole me before I can be a good me to a life partner."

Grace summed up, "The post-divorce bucket list is an opportunity to grow into yourself so that, if and when you do find a life partner, that person falls in love with and is a good match for the confident and secure you." For Grace, "It is an opportunity to finally engage my own agency in the world."

Taking a risk certainly paid off for these ladies. Luckily, the only ticket you need to win this life lottery is your signed divorce decree!

Twenty Three

Document Your Divorce

This may sound peculiar, but I'll always cherish the anxiety-filled, tearful moments I spent alone in my backyard journaling during the divorce process. In the end, I found peace. Even now when I sit outside, I reflect on those days. Screaming on paper helped me release emotions and face honesty. Though at the time, I kept those thoughts private, many young divorcées choose to publish their journeys online.

Most notable is Kensie, founder of a popular divorced-before-30 blog. She began posting about her divorce and even compiled her entries into a memoir. The now happily re-married mother of two told me, "When I decided to write a book about my experience, I had an eight-month-old baby and a full-time job, so I wasn't sure how I would find the time. I decide to publish the first draft as what I called a 'blogoir' (blog meets memoir). So I plotted out the story and broke it into bite-sized pieces. Every four or five days for nine months, I posted another piece of the story. Unlike a typical blog, it was an ongoing narrative. I didn't finish the story online, though. After the nine months, I unplugged and began editing and finishing the storyline."

Kensie continued, "When I started writing, I was really excited. I had a ton of energy to throw into the project. By the end, I felt exhausted but satisfied. The most interesting part of the process was having people read drafts of my manuscript. My friends, family members, and writing group members saw things I couldn't have seen, and this led to lots of interesting discussions and, in fact, closer relationships."

The fact that she found love again didn't hinder her efforts. Actually, her new husband was very supportive of the endeavor. "He has been one of my most helpful readers. In fact, he encouraged me to share more than I was initially comfortable sharing. I think that writing the book has been really good for our relationship, too. It seems crazy, but it's true!"

Now in her 30s, the Minnesota native has discovered a few things. "I learned how to be more open than I ever thought imaginable. Did I ever dream that my parents and in-laws would be reading about my relationship and even my sex life? Um, no. But it's been really cool to be this transparent. The downsides have been outweighed by the rewards."

Rory from Massachusetts garnered a following by blogging about life as a divorced-before-30-mom.

"I was facing my 30th birthday and going through the second year of my first baby's life as a single, not-yet-divorced, mom and I needed an outlet. And fast, lest I wanted to also face a straight jacket," Rory told me. "During my marriage, I had learned about the process of divorce and even found the strength to leave by reading other divorce blogs and other women's stories all over the Internet. I figured, 'Hey, if you can't beat 'em then join 'em!'"

The experience played a vital role in helping her deal with divorce. "Not only have I been able to connect and network with other like-minded women out there in the blogsphere, but I've built a small community of support for others like me who have found themselves in a similar situation: married, divorced or still in the process of divorcing someone so completely wrong for them it is almost insane contemplating how you were in love enough to get married at one point."

Rory said blogging allowed her to thoroughly deconstruct, process and divulge just why she got married to the wrong person in the first place and to honestly face both his and her contribution to the eventual failure of their union. "This is the most treasured piece of what I take away from it because, as they say, if you don't understand history it is bound to repeat itself."

She credited blogging with helping her to achieve personal growth and considers it a blessing. "I never thought that through blogging I would meet so many people who understand what it is like to go through divorce so young and with young children, too. I am smarter and happier now."

While Rory blogged to connect with other divorced-before-30-mothers, Ariel from New Jersey kept a diary to sort through feelings after divorce interrupted her mommyhood dreams. Following our initial interview, Ariel kept me up to date by sending entries for publication. Though she had just entered a new relationship at the time, Ariel still dealt with divorce-related anxiety, which she documented.

Here are entries from Ariel's divorce diary:

August 1ˢᵗ
"I went on vacation this week to the same place I go every year with my family, including my sister and her boyfriend. The same place I used to go with my husband. I couldn't help but be sad at first getting there, remembering fun times we had, and feeling alone. I watched all the couples, and thought, 'that was me.' I am very happy that I no longer have to deal with my husband, but the memories are hard to let go. As the week progressed, I felt better about being there, but I can't help wonder if I will always feel this way...even if I am happy again."

August 8th

"I'm still going through the settlement stage of this divorce process. But here is what I don't get—my husband left me to move in with his parents, so why am I solely responsible for all the costs of the house myself? I'm drowning in debt while he lives comfortably at home. Oh, and he also just bought a brand new car. Gotta love it. So right now the last thing on my mind is him or how he's feeling. I hope my lawyer rips him a new one and he owes me everything he's not paying. I also just got my notice of my early settlement court date. And I have to get my house appraised. Honestly, if I knew this would happen, I would have been smarter about my money. There should be a book about what not to do when you get married in case of divorce! For instance, don't add your husband's name to your account, or buy a house in just your name. This week has been stressful and it's not moving forward at all."

August 15th

"I called to get my house appraised, so I can get this thing rolling. The only problem is that the last time I talked to my lawyer, he said my husband's lawyer was taking his sweet time and that's why things were moving so slowly. Plus, every time they send back a new offer, it coincides with the one previously sent. Example: he wants all of our tax return back. For whatever reason, he thinks he deserves it. On the first statement he said he wanted all of it, on the last statement he said he hasn't received his half. My lawyer called to tell him that he needs to get his shit together and figure out what they are really asking for. There goes another week of nothing. Plus, I am a teacher, and my summer job is making it hard to keep up with all of the bills on our house. My parents actually had to pay my mortgage for August, otherwise I would have a hell of a late fee (and then some) to pay. And I love how while I am still struggling to stay afloat, my ex-husband is throwing cash away at casinos in Pennsylvania. Fabulous. Just another reason to be so over and done with all of this!

As I write this, my sister's boyfriend asks me to go ring shopping with him. I am thrilled, but also sad. Everyone around me is again becoming engaged, married, or pregnant, and I am starting over. It's hard to swallow thinking how my life would have been now if we were still happy and married, although I don't think we would have been able to be happy. Too many outside things were just working against us. Plus, I knew we were both falling out of love, so it worked out for the best. Now I am so much happier, and if it takes five years to remarry and have kids, then it does. At least I know I will be happy and life will be better.

On the plus side, I am becoming more open to going places with my new boy and no longer caring who I see. Because I am so happy and enjoying our time together, it doesn't bother me if someone questions it."

August 22nd

"The house appraisal is on Thursday, which is also the same day I am going to help my sister's boyfriend pick out engagement rings. I also received another packet from my husband's lawyer about more stuff I have to fill out to prove my earnings. So now I have 15 days to fill out this large packet of paperwork and make copies of required statements. OMG...really? I called my lawyer because this is taking way too long and he said that my husband's lawyer has not been getting back to him. Convenient, right? Now I'm just getting pissed that this lawyer is making my life hell. It never ends. I keep hoping that no matter what happens I get back every cent of mortgage he hasn't paid. If I don't, at least I'm rid of him. I'm feeling so defeated right now because I am just so far in debt while he is cruising around in a new car, that it's hard to think about the final outcome.

I did have an awesome weekend with my new boy at Hershey Park. Just being around him brightens my day. I'm happy I found someone who could do that, because the last was far from it! It's nice to feel so cared about and just know how right this divorce is—I could not be happier in my decision!

The new school year starts, and I went back to my maiden name, so I have to go change all the paperwork for my classroom. I'm not really looking forward to the awkward questions from parents of former students. But hey, that's life. What can you do?"

September 7th

"My sister will be engaged this weekend. I am very happy for her and can't wait to take part in her planning process. I remember how fun and stressful it was. It makes me think of all the 'good' things that came with marriage, before all the bad took over. So this month it also happens to be my birthday, and I have to say turning 29 is making me stress a bit. I had a totally different plan for this point in my life, and all is different—good different—but again, I freak about being too old to have children, and blah...the usual stuff you think about when you are 'single' turning 29."

September 18th

"My sister got engaged and I am very happy for her. Now the wedding planning will begin. I have to say that the past week I've been very happy with where my life is going and I love my new guy. Everyday I stop and think about how much happier I am with the way my life is going, but my birthday is this upcoming Wednesday and I keep telling everyone that it is my un-birthday. Something about turning 29 is scary. But, I'm going to embrace it as the best year yet, since I am no longer under my ex's rules and can celebrate and be who I am! Although, the one thing I really do want for my birthday is a divorce!"

October 10th

"I went to a coworker's wedding this weekend. It was a little harder to get through than I thought. Listening to the vows and the meanings behind the rings kinda made me think of what they never

meant to him (or me). It's also hard knowing everyone around me is married now, or getting married, and life is starting over for me, they are all experiencing what I did once have. I guess it just feels weird. I never once regret my decision because I am happy now where I am, it's just odd to be the one on the outside now."

October 31st

"This Wednesday we go to court for our early settlement panel and my lawyer has said that I could possibly be officially divorced in a few weeks. I still don't understand how my ex-husband is not responsible for any mortgage payments when I have been doing it all, and yet I still have to pay him to keep it. The laws of divorce are clearly insane. I have to say, I am so nervous to be going into court. This will be the first time that I will see him in months and it will be so weird. I have also been crying a lot over what I am losing on the house and having no money. I feel like I am going to lose it in this mediation hearing. It just seems like I've had so much built up emotion that seeing him and his clear lack of respect will send me over the edge. I also found out that he is seeing someone new. It's just a weird thing to hear and think about."

November 2nd

"Well, it's official! I signed my divorce papers! I am a free woman and it feels great. I am so happy to finally have this done. The only thing I need to worry about now is what to do with the house once I get the appraisal back. Walking out of the courthouse with my lawyer, sun shining down, I felt a huge relief and stress lifted off my shoulders. Now onto wonderful bigger and better things! I am so throwing myself a divorce party!"

December 11th

"A few weeks ago I adopted a dog and she's great. I have been crating her because she has bad separation anxiety and can be a bit destructive. The other day, she managed to get out of her crate and proceeded to destroy a box in the closet. As I looked through the

stuff, I realized she destroyed my box full of wedding pictures and mementos. Out of all the boxes she chose that one. Coincidence? I don't think so. I was holding off for some reason about getting rid of them, so she made it that much easier to throw it all away. I think she was definitely the dog that was meant for me."

Ariel had her divorce party, as you read about earlier in this book. Her boyfriend also moved in, so she was able to keep her house. Everything worked out in the end! And because women like Kensie, Rory, and Ariel document their struggles and successes, we are able to pass that knowledge on to the new generation of divorcées.

Twenty Four

Shape Up

L ace up those sneakers, it's time to hit the pavement. No excuses! Health and wellness should be one of your top post-
divorce priorities. If you hate exercise, bribe yourself by going
shopping for cute workout gear. Consider it shopping for your
health!

Whether or not you sought comfort in carbs or dropped to a skel-
etal version of yourself, chances are your body needs a little TLC.

Shape up and knock 'em dead. When you feel amazing inside,
it will show through your appearance. It'll also bring confidence
to get back on the dating scene or maybe apply for a new job.

It worked for Sydney from Florida. A survivor of abuse, she learned
through legitimate sweat and tears. "A lot of attention is paid to the
external injuries inflicted by abuse—the bruises, the broken bones,
the concussions. What often goes unremarked upon is the way abuse
corrodes your insides, how it eats away at your confidence and your
spirit until you are little more than a husk of your former self."

Sydney confided, "When I left, I was haunted by something
that bears a strong resemblance to post-traumatic stress disorder.
I ground my teeth in my sleep and woke up with my jaw aching.

Several times a week, I slept, only to face nightmares of humiliation and pain. My anxiety attacks subsided, but they were replaced by the certainty that I would come back to my apartment one day to find him hiding inside my shower. Mundane household chores reminded me of things he said or did, and I'd find myself curled in a ball on the floor, screaming silently into my hands."

At first, Sydney turned to substances for quick fixes. "They smoothed over my jagged edges and helped me sleep, but they wouldn't do for the long term. Not if I wanted to get past bare-knuckle survival, or if I wanted to learn how to thrive."

Then, post-divorce, she went for her first run. "My boyfriend, who is now my husband, was a recovering alcoholic who had taken up marathons in his quest for wellness," Sydney explained. "I wasn't an alcoholic or an addict, just someone with some bad habits, but the parallels between our lives and the self-destructive choices we had made were unmistakable. So when he spoke of the way running had transformed him, I listened. One day, I laced up a pair of trainers, put on a pair of terry-cloth shorts and a cotton tank top, and I headed out for a short run with him. I made it all of a block before my tar-clogged lungs and my weak calves started screaming for mercy."

Though Sydney could have easily quit, she pushed herself to the limit. "Sometimes I felt wretched, all sweaty, sore and clumsy. Sometimes I threw up. Sometimes I put off my runs until the sun was high in the air, and then I used the heat as an excuse to stay inside my air-conditioned apartment. But then, sometimes, against everything logical and reasonable in the universe, it felt wonderful."

Eventually, she built up her endurance and even completed a 5K marathon, followed by a 12K! Running gave Sydney the confidence to conquer other out-there goals, like public speaking, which led to a new job.

"This sea of courage was inside of me all along, an unused resource just waiting to be tapped. Running gave me a safe, controlled way to do that. I realized that I was stronger than I'd ever suspected, that I was more fearless than I'd ever imagined. That knowledge has bled into every part of my life," concluded Sydney.

Fellow survivor of abuse and running advocate, Rachel from Maryland said the activity "relieved stress and made me feel better about myself."

Rachel noted, "I read statistics of how not many women get out of physically and mentally abusive relationships and the numbers are grim but I did it! If I can do this, then anyone can!"

In honor of her strength, Rachel nourished her neglected appearance by getting a haircut, buying new clothes and beginning a diet. "I let my hair grow out and put in layers; I curled it and fixed it when I went out. When I was with my ex-husband I never did that. Now, I go to the gym, eat healthier and I go out with friends—something that I never used to do because he never liked it when I wasn't at his beck and call."

While Rachel pampered herself, Justine from New York took a mud bath—just not the relaxing spa version. "I signed up for my first twelve-mile obstacle course a week after I left him and a month and a half after, I completed it. It was a rush," exclaimed Justine. "I have done three since and just signed up for my fourth."

Belle from Indiana pushed herself to new limits by adapting more of a vegetarian/vegan diet after leaving her junk food loving husband. "I've always been into the healthier side and am pretty daring about trying new things," she said. "It's really easy this past year to just not eat, but I have always loved my fruits and veggies. Even if I just throw some spinach, different fruits, ice, and natural fruit juices in a blender for breakfast or at work."

Embracing a healthier lifestyle led Mae from Massachusetts to lose 60 pounds. Though she said her changes were slow but drastic, Mae lost 40 pounds in one year and the final 20 after she sold her car and began walking everywhere. "I feel amazing and can't remember the last time I felt this healthy and happy," she proclaimed.

Long gone are her days of debauchery. "During my marriage, I was so depressed that I started drinking a lot," Mae admitted.

"When I left him, the depression started to melt away, and I quit smoking, stopped drinking every night, and began to exercise almost daily. I started off by walking my niece in her carriage every day, then I built up to jogging a little bit, and this past summer I ran my first 5K road race!"

Eating healthier, observing caloric intake, and practicing yoga also contributed to her new slim silhouette. "It was a long journey," said Mae, "so don't get discouraged if you don't see immediate results," she warned.

On the other hand, Lucy from Texas is watching the weight drop off after adopting natural supplements into her regime. "I lost 14.7 lbs and two inches in 24 days and gained a lifetime of energy," Lucy stated of her progress thus far.

"I am almost 28 years old and after getting re-married four years ago, I went from a size 8 to a size 18," revealed Lucy. She admitted, "I was the girl who always had an energy drink or cup of coffee in her hand at meetings, outside when getting my nicotine fix, or pretty much doing anything that involved walking! I was addicted to chemical energy and my diet was anything I could grab on the go. I would never spend money on a monthly gym membership because I always found excuses for other ways to spend that money."

Then, Lucy started her 24-day challenge, replacing her go-to energy drinks and coffee with a sugar-free, vitamin packed supplement. "I ran with this product and never looked back! I loved it. I was awake, but not jittery and I was losing weight by taking vitamins!"

Now that she has jump-started her weight loss, Lucy said, "I have more energy and motivation to make better food choices and even make my workout—house cleaning, laundry, etc.—work for me!"

From old school exercise to vitamin supplements, there are endless options for health and wellness practices. No matter which method you use, make sure you're doing so for the right reasons.

Marriage was a legal pledge to your partner. Divorce is commitment to become the best version of you, emotionally and physically. It's important to acknowledge that women don't need to be skinny to be beautiful and many skinny women are not healthy or happy. So love who you are in the process. Celebrating your health and wellness by shaping up requires hard work and dedication. Believe in yourself and chase those finish lines and goals. One day, you'll wake up brand new.

Twenty Five

Get Engaged...In New Social Activities!

S ay 'yes' to the invitation. That's 27-year-old law student Carly's advice to recent divorcées.

Whether it's for a simple girl's night out, a dinner with friends or a drink after work, say 'yes.' Even if you're tired, bummed or burnt out, say 'yes.' Carly followed that very formula to post-divorce bliss.

"Divorce can be painful, scary, and draining," she noted during our interview. "Even when it's what we wanted, it's still hard to get up and get dressed some mornings. It sometimes seems easier to hide away from the world at home in our jammies and lick our wounds and preserve our dignity."

Carly continued, "I go out with friends all the time. When I was married, I hardly ever went out with friends. My ex would always berate or guilt me into staying home and waiting for him, and then he never showed up. Once we separated, I began going out more. I started saying 'yes' to the people who I always said 'no' to. Thank God I have a great group of friends who kept asking when I was married even when they knew I would say 'no!'"

Here's Carly's Just Say 'Yes' Guide:

- Start by going out with your girlfriends. Keep it low key if you're more comfortable with that at first—a small dinner or drinks at someone's house.
- After saying 'yes' to small gatherings at home, it gets easier to say 'yes' to big things like an evening out.
- Even when things don't go quite as planned—go with it.
- Even if your date cancels—say 'yes.'
- Even if you feel fat or can't find the perfect shoes—say 'yes.'

"Learning to go with the flow is part of divorce, and learning to sit with something that is uncomfortable helps us grow into the women we were meant to become," she advised.

Carly affirmed, "Saying 'yes' allowed me to grow as a person and as a woman—to meet people and do things I never would have done otherwise. Sure, sometimes I drink too much or feel awkward because I'd forgotten what it was like to go out in groups. But at the end of the night, no matter how amazing or awful the experience was, I leave with a smile on my face because I said 'yes,' not just to going out, but to living wonderful."

Molly from Massachusetts got cooking when she said 'yes' to new social activities. "When I got divorced, one of the great pieces of advice I got was, 'Don't stay inside, make sure you get out of the house and do things with other people,'" Molly said, noting, "I also really badly wanted to conquer things I always wanted to do but never felt I had the time. Now I was living my life for me and me only, so I found the perfect activity. It not only helped me get out of the house and meet new people, but it also gave me a skill set that will benefit me one day if I'm ever in another relationship."

Thus, Molly's decision to participate in cooking classes. "I couldn't help but think in the back of my head that having some skills in the kitchen wouldn't be a bad thing if I met a guy, so that is why I initially started," she admitted. "What I realized was it was a great way to interact with a whole new group of people—including some single guys, surprise, surprise—and not sit on the couch at night and sulk."

Molly has taken courses in cake decorating, appetizers, brunch, soups, Italian sauces, and pizza dough. "I plan to keep taking them, as well." She reported, "The classes are interactive and I was comfortable going to them alone and making new friends. I would bring the leftover food into work the next day and continue all the positive interaction with my coworkers while we discussed the class and what I learned."

The classes made Molly feel independent and good about something she had to offer. "It was the perfect way to celebrate my divorce," said Molly. "It is never a bad thing to know your way around the kitchen. It is easy to impress around the holidays, coworkers think you are fabulous, and a new man will inevitably be thrilled that his girl can cook. These are all positive things, which is exactly what you need when celebrating your divorce."

Here is one of Molly's favorite recipes she learned in class:

Moroccan Chickpea and Parsley Soup

Ingredients:
  2 cups drained chickpeas (canned is good, or cook raw ones)
  1 large onion
  1 handful parsley
  Olive oil
  1 teaspoon ground cumin
  1 teaspoon tahini paste (ground sesame seeds)
  5-6 cups of chicken stock
  Juice of 1 lemon
  Salt and pepper to taste

Steps:

Sauté the onion and chopped parsley in the olive oil until the onion softens. Scrape into the soup pot. Add the chickpeas, stock, tahini paste, and cumin. Bring to a simmer and cook 15-20 minutes. Purée the soup with a hand mixer or blender (with a paper towel over the small opening in the lid). Add the lemon juice, season with salt and pepper, and serve.

Now that you're hungry, eat up this advice from Carly: "Three little letters—Y-E-S, probably changed my life more than I-D-O."

Twenty Six

Take a Selfie

W hen you deleted your ex-husband from your life, chances are your virtual world suffered a devastating loss: a ton of pictures in which you looked amazing. Your online profile is most likely in desperate need of a "face" lift. This calls for a divorcette photo shoot. These snapshots can also be used to create an online dating profile, so you'll want to make sure you look your best!

Fellow divorcée and photographer extraordinaire, Leanne from New Mexico stated, "We all know that having flattering photographs of yourself on your profile is the most effective way to draw interested individuals in to learn more about you. Having good, quality photographs on your online profile seemed self-explanatory to me at first; however, I learned a lot about successful strategies through this new process."

Here are Leanne's tips for breathtaking profile pictures:

Lighting is key. "When you decide to take some new photographs for your profile, pick a sunny day. There is nothing more attractive than natural sunlight on your face. The sunlight will highlight your best features and make your photographs look stunning. Have a friend go outside with you or set your timer on your camera while you soak up some rays outside. If you insist on taking photographs of yourself inside, try to avoid the flash. The flash on your camera will more than likely flatten your face and make you appear ghostly. Pick a room with lots of incandescent light or better yet, sunlight, to take some self-portraits."

Nix the pics with your ex. "We all have the old pictures with our ex's arms around us—please don't use these old photographs in your profile. Go take some new pictures! It's easy and can be a lot of fun to take new self-portraits. Also, you don't want to bring that baggage to a new friendship. Plus, it's just tacky!"

Ditch the sunglasses! "I can't tell you how many profiles I've seen where the individual is wearing sunglasses in every photo! Your eyes are the window into your soul, so show off your eyes in your photos! We can't gauge anything about how you look if you are wearing sunglasses in your profile picture—show off your face! There's nothing wrong with having some photos of you outside or engaging in activities with other people, but your main profile picture should showcase your face."

Only use current pictures. "One friend I made through online dating told me a horror story of a girl that had used photos from years ago in her profile. Imagine his surprise when he met her and she looked nothing like what she claimed online! It's really not that hard to take photographs. You probably have a camera on your phone to do so! Only post current pictures from the last six months so your profile is flattering and honest."

Don't try to fool anyone. "I have a horror story myself. I had dinner with a gentleman that I met online and didn't recognize him at the restaurant because the photos on his profile were totally bogus! People will find out eventually if your photos are not you, obviously. It's best to be honest in your profile and don't try to fool your new friends! If you lie about your photographs, what else are you lying about?"

Frequently change your profile picture. "I've noticed that when I change my profile picture on dating sites, I get tons more hits! Sometimes a certain photograph may repel certain individuals when they are quickly window-shopping. If you change it up, someone who passed you up might give you a more careful look. I have a psychotherapist friend that said to me about online dating, 'Men often have a specific quality or preconception of the mate that they are looking for, so if someone passes you up, it doesn't mean you are not beautiful. It just means you do not fit that mold that the individual has created for their mate.' It's important to keep your profile up to date and switch up those photos to bring more people in!"

Take advantage of editing tools. "There's really no 'wrong' way to take self-portraits for your profile. You can use your webcam, phone camera or SLR camera to take your photo. Be aware of your lighting. There's only so much you can fix in a photo-editing program if you have poor lighting.

If you have a photo-editing program (you can even download free apps on your phone), you can crop and change the look and feel of your photos after you shoot. Don't alter your photos too much. It's fairly obvious when someone has altered a photograph and it can hinder any trust between you and your viewer.

I often do minor changes with my photographs: I will crop out any junk in the background, adjust the levels of the photo to increase contrast and even out the tones, and adjust the hue/saturation if the photo has too much red or green tint to it. Then, I will save it as a smaller size so it loads faster on mobile devices."

Now that you have these tips, strike a pose! Just beware of posting too many selfies. It's way more appealing to see photos of you out and about with friends having a great time. However you capture it, with great profile picture and open mind, the adventure can begin.

Twenty Seven

Fall in Love Again

Welcome to the jungle, ladies. Navigating the dating scene post-divorce can be far from fun, at least when you first set out on the prowl.

Bethany from Ohio has been through the downfalls. "I was once talked into doing speed dating. It was a horrible experience. I enjoy meeting new people but it seemed so rushed (by definition, I guess). I also had to 'date' people I could have gone my entire life without meeting. I asked one guy what he does and his reply was, 'I hoop, play video games, eat.' I'm like, 'No...what do you do for a living...?'"

Even when dates are firmly set, evenings can end up rather soggy. Take the experience of Emily from North Carolina, for instance. One guy took her on a first date to a hot dog stand. No, the carnival wasn't in town. But perhaps there was a circus over in Michigan missing a clown because participant Gwen definitely encountered a man with some behavioral problems who was clearly not her "match."

Gwen recounted, "The morning I paid my subscription to a dating site, a man messaged me immediately. After exchanging several rapid emails, he asked for my phone number. I figured, 'Why not?' He called me a few minutes later and we were having a lovely time talking about our jobs when I heard a strange noise. I continued chatting with him but kept hearing odd noises. Finally, I asked him if everything was all right, at which point he admitted he was 'edging,' aka masturbating. I hung up."

Yikes. That's hardly the ideal post-divorce sexual experience. But there's always worse. Like the old high school friend with whom Lucy from Texas attempted to hit the sheets.

"We went on several dates, but nothing physical because it was too soon for me," shared Lucy. "We kissed about three weeks in and after about three months, we attempted to 'have relations.' He was a bouncer type with large muscles," Lucy pointed out, but to her disappointment, that's all that was large.

To set the scene, Lucy's suitor put on florescent lights and cheesy music. She continued, "He expected me to get straight naked and loose all inhibitions. That was awkward. He left to go get protection in the next room and came back 15 minutes later! That threw me off. And even though the condom was still in the wrapper, unopened, I could instantly smell latex on him. It was that awful smell that I didn't understand. I thought, 'What did he do, go try it on for size first?'"

Then, Lucy decided she had to peace out of his place. "I was introduced to his naked body to find that he was really small. He was all muscle except for that area. I thought maybe he just needed to 'grow up.' But no, it was the size of a marker cap! And he said he was ready for action. He tried to stand there proudly, like 'look what I got' and I just started laughing. I couldn't help it."

To think, all that time Lucy was feeling self-conscious! "I tried to hold it back, but I busted out laughing, which he took as a turn on, like I was laughing with him, not at him."

Next, Lucy said, "He got on me and started to kiss me. I quickly took my palm, pressed it on his forehead and pushed gently so he would get off of me before that 'thumb' got anywhere close to me. He took the hint and asked what was wrong. Did he really not know? I told him I was not ready and went outside to smoke a cigarette." Lucy put out both flames and went home.

Situations like those above often leave divorcées discouraged, but for some spirits are dampened even before the first date.

After ending her nine-year relationship, my bestie Penny is finding out the hard way. "How to meet people has changed since I was last looking for love; now it's all about online dating, which I'm not into," she sighed during a recent conversation.

Through the interview process, I've found young divorcées have mixed feelings about meeting men online. But most agree it's worth a shot. For one thing, you get to state upfront in your profile that you're divorced. Another bonus? You can search for men in a similar situation. Perhaps there's single dad just waiting for a mother figure to stumble upon his profile. If all else fails, it's a great way to relearn how to date. Practicing on the "wrong" guys will prepare you for when Mr. Right walks into your life.

One online dating success story comes from 29-year-old Gabriella from Florida.

"It had been only a short time after my divorce and I was still trying to heal," Gabriella said about her membership decision. "I was basically using online dating as a tool to build my self-esteem and keep myself distracted."

She quickly learned the pros and cons of online courtship. "A lot of men contacted me so I would have a lot of emails to read on a daily basis," Gabriella told me. "Even though there were a variety of men, a lot of them seemed to be more interested in a physical relationship or just the opposite, they wanted someone to settle down with and I was not interested. Sometimes I would receive emails saying how pretty or beautiful I was, and let's face it, after a divorce it's nice to hear things like that from the opposite sex."

Gabriella kept her real life private, so she controlled all communication. "Sometimes they would want your Facebook information and then they would Facebook stalk you," she noted.

After two weeks of talking online, Gabriella moved one relationship from the virtual to the real world. She daringly met her crush make-up free by a pool. Gabriella recalled the moment she first watched him walk towards her: "He was tall, had a nice build, beautiful blue eyes and a southern accent. I remember thinking to myself, 'I have never dated a southern boy.' I am Puerto Rican and Cuban and most of the men I've dated have been minorities."

Gabriella had been slightly anxious as to his reaction. "I am overweight, and due to the fact that my husband had left me for a skinnier, younger woman, you could say that it was a huge blow to my self-esteem."

The pair talked for hours. Before they parted, Gabriella asked, "So I am not too big for you?" and with a smile, he bent down to hug her and said, "No, you're perfect." They've been together ever since.

Awwww! Adorable right? Wait, there are more tales of happily even after divorce by way of online dating, continuing with Liv from Pennsylvania.

"After being married, I didn't want to jump into another serious relationship, but to have a little fun," shared Liv. "I wanted to go out with different guys and try different things."

Therefore, Liv ventured online and rejoined multiple dating sites. That's when she met her boyfriend. "We're taking it slow and not rushing the relationship but I love sleeping next to him at night and waking up to him in the morning," she admitted. "Not a day has gone by since that he doesn't make me laugh or smile. It has also opened my eyes to what I was missing in my marriage. I very much look forward to seeing where this relationship goes."

Considering online dating? Take Liv's advice:

1. "Common sense, common sense, common sense! I created a separate email address to use for online dating purposes, that way in case anything goes south, the person doesn't have my real email. Also, all the spam that comes with online dating sites doesn't clog my other account."

2. "If you feel you want to meet someone, always meet in a public space at a busy time, and come in your own car and leave in your own car. Give yourself time to feel this person out."

3. "I always told a girlfriend where I was going and how long I expected to be gone. She would text me during the date to make sure I was OK. We also had a safe word. This is important in case the date is a bust or you need an out. Make sure the word is something you wouldn't use in an everyday conversation like 'moosetracks,' 'dinosaur,' or 'starfish.' A quick trip to the ladies room, to send off a text and you could have an out in no time flat. The buddy system is big and gives you a safety net. I know that dating online is so common these days but that doesn't mean there still aren't weirdos out there."

Online dating sites aren't the only virtual outlets to mate-up. Don't forget about good 'ol Facebook. Changing your status from "married" to "single" can release flocks of suitors. But first, you need the courage to put yourself out there and publicly announce your divorce.

"That part was terrible," admitted Liz from Massachusetts. "I went 'inactive' on Facebook for a couple months and when I re-activated my profile, there wasn't a single mention of him, like he never existed. I took down all the pictures and just kind of acted like it never happened."

Sara from Egypt agreed, "The status change was hard, because I didn't want to publicize anything—I was in shock still at the time. He, on the other hand, changed his status from 'married' to 'single' and 'interested in women' one week later. I kept my status as married for a few weeks. Then, I felt like I was so mad that I used to be married to a person like that, so I've removed the status entirely from my page."

Like Liz and Sara, Grace from Pennsylvania went incognito. "I deactivated my Facebook account for a while and when I reactivated it I just eliminated the 'relationship status' category altogether, which does not show up on people's news feeds and is not very conspicuous. Unless someone is really paying close attention to your profile—in which case they are kind of a stalker and have their own problems—no one even notices. In fact, there are Facebook friends with whom I have not talked in years who probably still think I am married."

On the contrary, Hadley from New York exclaimed, "I couldn't wait to change my last name back on Facebook. It's scary that life has come to that, but I felt that my status change and name change via social media was more important than the actual divorce decree!"

Juniper from Oklahoma sided with Hadley. "It was liberating. It got a lot of reaction; emails and texts started pouring in. That was a very defining moment. It separated my real friends—people who showed up where I was staying with bottles of wine and plenty of time to talk—from my fake friends—people who emailed me wanting to know what happened and all the juicy details."

Clara from New Jersey reconnected with an old crush on Facebook and the rest, as they say, is history. "Two weeks prior to my ex-husband leaving, my best friend from high school returned to town because his mother had passed away. A little back-story: we had been best friends and his mother always wanted us together. When we were 20, he got married. However, the night before he married his now ex-wife, he kissed me and told me he had and will always love me. I had always loved him and was heartbroken when he told me that he loved me and married her the next day."

His marriage lasted a mere ten months. But by then, Clara was involved with her future ex-husband. So when her high school bff (who we'll refer to as Romeo), returned and professed his love, Clara said, "I was hurt and confused. He asked me to run away with him. I told him I couldn't."

They didn't speak for many years after that, but Clara admitted, "I always thought of him. I always missed him and never stopped loving him."

Fast forward to the weeks before Clara's divorce, where she ran into Romeo. "It was like a scene from a movie. Everything slowed down. The world was moving in slow motion. His eyes met mine and my heart ached. My pulse quickened. My hands got clammy. We hugged each other and I didn't want to let go. He told me his mom had died. I felt horrible. We went our separate ways that day and a couple weeks later, my husband left."

A week later, Romeo sent Clara a friend request on Facebook. "I accepted. We chatted and he told me he still loved me. My ex had only been gone a week; my heart was a mirror image of what it was a few years prior. I hid how I really felt and ignored obvious signs my ex wasn't for me. Now, here I was, certain that I loved Romeo, but feeling like I should hide those feelings because of what others might say. I didn't care anymore. I told him I loved him. He visited me and when I was in his arms I never wanted to leave. His love made me safe, confident, beautiful, happy and secure."

Clara introduced Romeo to her son from a previous relationship, who was having problems learning to speak. "He wasn't talking at all. Not a single word. Doctors sent him to specialists. They tested him for autism. No one could tell me why he wasn't talking," informed Clara.

Clara's son and Romeo clicked immediately and soon, Romeo moved into their home. Then, a miracle happened. Clara's son called Romeo "daddy!" Turns out all he needed was a safe, happy environment to flourish. Romeo adopted Clara's son after they married. The newlyweds recently welcomed a baby girl, whom they named after Romeo's mother. "We honestly believe it was one of her first duties as an angel to bring us back together," Clara surmised.

Well if that story doesn't make you tear up, then I don't know what will! Making yourself available online can change your life, but don't rule out meeting the man of your dreams while you're out and about.

Emily from North Carolina told me, "The guy I'm currently seeing was actually my personal banker when my husband and I were splitting up! He helped me open a new account and we became friends."

Brooke from Wisconsin's post-divorce dating story is one of birds of a feather flocking together. She told me, "I met a random guy at a bar one night while out with the girls. We exchanged numbers and proceeded to talk and text for a few weeks. Finally we made plans to meet up one night. We met at a bar with groups of our respective friends. At some point in the night he leaned in and says, "I have to tell you something..."

Brooke, who had yet to reveal that she was in the process of divorcing, looked right back at him and said, "I should probably tell you something too, but you can go first." Looking rather sheepish, the guy proceeded to tell Brooke that he was married, but not really because he was in the middle of a divorce!

"I just started laughing and he looked at me like I had lost my mind," recalled Brooke, who also came clean. He ended up being her one-night stand guy. "We just had too much going on in our lives," Brooke concluded.

Harper from Arizona made it a point to date a diverse array of men after her divorce. "Younger, older, jobless, well-off, single dads, men who were divorced, men with no kids...not to make myself sound like a hoochie, because I certainly wasn't," Harper affirmed. "Some of these were literally one-time dates, and I never saw these men again. But it gave me the opportunity to see what was out there, and really find out what I did and didn't want in a partner."

And when she found that man, Blue Eyes if you recall, Harper said, "There were never any telltale things that I felt until well into the relationship. But I remember early on, we were sitting on his couch talking and getting to know each other, and he stated one of the things he really wanted in life was to one day have a daughter. He had two sons already from his previous marriage, so I asked if it was because he wanted to have the boy vs. girl experience. He said 'No, not really.' It was because he had always dreamed of one day walking his little girl down the aisle at her wedding. That melted my heart right then and there, and I was pretty much sold on him."

Finding love again can cause anxiety about marriage 2.0 because a divorcée doesn't want to make the same "mistake" again. You might find yourself looking for a sign that the man you're involved with is actually the right husband. But sometimes, you just have to trust your instincts.

Harlowe from Virginia didn't have a defining moment when she met her second husband. "I just trusted that it felt right and that we were both committed to seeing this through and working on our relationship, no matter what came along. I don't know if there is a 'one' or if it is just a matter of two people sticking to their commitment and keeping the communication lines open and trusting each other. That is something that I think about a lot, still."

Even Dr. Patricia Leavy didn't necessarily think her husband was "the one" when they first met. But, she said, "There was never a day, since then, that we didn't email, speak or see each other. We fell in love quickly but took the time and care to build a really strong partnership. He surprised me on vacation in Belgium with a proposal. I screamed, 'Yes!' at top of my lungs."

Caroline from Nevada has her first husband to thank for confirming her confidence in her second. "During the five years total I spent with my first husband, he never cared to take me to Puerto Rico, where I'm from, because it was 'too expensive' to fly there. My now-husband took me to Puerto Rico a year after we started dating, because he wanted to see where I came from. We've been there three times since we've been together."

Every twenty-something divorcée has the opportunity to find love again and while love can't be forced, it can certainly be strategized.

Allow me to suggest some post-divorce dating guidelines:

Don't talk about your ex-husband. It's acceptable to note you're happily divorced. But don't divulge any more details unless your date inquires. Instead, spend your time getting to know the man sitting across the table.

Don't put all your eggs in one basket. Now is your time to date around. Have (safe) fun and keep all your options open. Don't settle down unless you happen to meet the man who meets all the requirements on your dating checklist.

Branch out from your "type." If you've spent all your time chasing the same type of guy and keep ending up alone and annoyed at your situation, then it's time to reevaluate your game plan. Give the dorky guy next door a chance. He might have a killer body under that collared shirt and chances are he will worship the ground on which you walk. Come on, being wined and dined by a man who you know isn't sexting five other girls behind your back is certainly worth a shot!

Let him make the moves. Do not text or call the guy after your date. Let me repeat that, do not text or call the guy after your date. Besides the fact that you don't want to appear desperate, if he is genuinely interested in you, he *will* contact you. He has your phone number, email, social networking account, etc. There is no reason that a man will not want to contact you in the days following your date unless he is playing the field or not interested. In that case, move on. The man who is worth your time and energy will immediately prove his intentions.

Now you're armed with the tools for navigating the post-divorce dating jungle. What are you waiting for? Take off the camouflage you've been wearing for security, slip into a pair of heels and hunt down the love you deserve! There will be mishaps along the way, but look on the bright side: you'll have great stories to tell and each encounter with the wrong guy will make you appreciate the right one when he enters your life.

Twenty Eight

Where We Belong

By now, my dear divorcées, you have proof that closing the door on misery creates opportunity. It may have taken almost four years since I last walked out of my condo, but that other door eventually opened. When I turned the handle, it revealed hundreds of pink, white and red rose petals on my bedroom floor, a bouquet of red roses, and "Joelle, will you marry me?" spelled out in rose petals on the bed. That's how Frank asked me to be his wife.

It was a Thursday afternoon—June 28th to be exact. I came home from work, opened the bedroom door and in shock, put my hand over my mouth. Not only was I standing in the middle of my own private rose garden, but Frank also posted 54 heart-shaped notes around the room. Each described something he loves about me, from the way I 'tawk" and my love for our "dawgs," to how long it takes me to get ready for bed at night. I was so impressed by how much creativity Frank put into setting the scene that I don't even remember what he said as he slid the ring on my finger.

It was something along the lines of how he wanted to propose to me earlier and even considered asking me while we were on a romantic getaway at his family's shore house the prior week. However, he honored my wishes when I told him that he could not propose unless the planets were properly aligned.

Let me explain. I knew Frank was going to pop the question soon because we picked out the ring. Frank had been on diamond duty for months, but nothing caught his eye and I wanted to try on different settings, so I joined the hunt. While casually browsing, my eyes locked on a vintage-inspired, marquis-shaped, halo-set diamond. Throwing all plans of a princess-cut stone out the window, we handed the saleswoman a credit card and went home 99 percent engaged. The date was May 11th, which fell on the luckiest weekend of the year according to noted astrologer, Susan Miller. Ironically, I didn't plan the purchase. However, it's good to know luck is on my side this time!

There was another omen, too. When we got in the car to drive home, one of my favorite 80s love songs came on the radio. We never listen to the radio but played it that night and a swoon-worthy song I love but hadn't heard on the radio for years just happened to be on rotation. Fate?

Once we had the ring, I told Frank he had to tweet Susan Miller and inquire the best astrological time for engagement. She had previously reported that it's not ideal to form unions when Mercury is in retrograde. For all I knew, the last time I got engaged or married, the planets had gone awry. This might explain a lot! Like a good future husband, Frank made a fake Twitter account and wrote Susan. He proposed on her first approved date.

Sure, I felt bad that I picked out my engagement ring and didn't have a completely surprising proposal, but that didn't take away from the moment.

Being engaged again—to a man I am confident is my soul mate—has been surreal. I waited so long for this to happen, wondering who my future husband would be, how we would meet and fall in love, that it's weird this is my life now.

Frank once told me not to feel bad about my past because we wouldn't be where we are without those days. He's right. I knew the night he sent a random text message, "We're perfect for each other by the way," that this was something special. Sometimes I can't believe I found someone who loves me like I love him. But then again, I'm awesome, so it's about time I met my equal!

In all seriousness, I'm definitely more at peace now that I have formal future plans. I know it will be a while before Frank and I will have children, but I've accepted the reality. Having a baby in my early 30s won't be the end of the world. Waiting (or being forced to wait) allowed me to truly experience life. I've had a blast indulging in my hobbies and dating a few of the wrong men through my days. It helped me appreciate my relationship with Frank. It's true, without great struggle there is no reward.

I'll never forget the nights I lay awake terrified of my situation. Set in panic mode, I pushed myself to the limits, and came to embrace freedom and sweat optimism from every pore. I ended up where I belong.

About two weeks after I got engaged, Penny, my appointed maid of honor, told me a bridal boutique near her house was having a $100 sample dress sale. I had been researching like crazy, from simple department store dresses to luxurious gowns. I didn't want to sacrifice my experience as a bride just because my first attempt backfired, but I needed affordable options. The sample sale sounded too good to be true. I went, expecting to be disappointed.

I ended up finding my dream dress—or so I thought! It was exactly what I wanted, but even better than I imagined. The sweetheart neckline and tulle ballgown met my requirements. The bejeweled bodice and breathtaking appliqué lace and flowers on the skirt were touches I didn't think I'd ever be able to afford. The only catch was that the dress—originally priced at $1,000—was sold "as is," about eight sizes too big and required alterations, but I'm used to making adjustments! I calculated that even if the alterations cost a few hundred dollars, I had scored a deal. I had already ordered a custom-made alencon lace and ostrich feather bolero adorned with a sparkly broach, so this would complete my vintage look.

I counted down the months until the bolero arrived in the mail, eager to try it on with my dress. When the moment finally arrived, something unexpected happened—I hated the dress! There was just too much going on between the beading, lace, flowers and layers of tulle, so I felt that the dress clashed with the shrug. On top of that, I didn't feel that spark. My body drowned in the heavy material, which I felt was meant for a fairytale-type bride. I had to pause and be honest with myself:

It's the marriage that matters when all is said and done, so does the dress really matter? It took me one second to decide that yes, it does! But, could I picture myself walking down the aisle in that frock? Or did I make an impulsive purchase because the price was right and I was stressing out about having to pay for a wedding? Was I so excited to be a bride again that I just couldn't wait to buy a dress? Did it actually enhance my body or just hide "problem" areas? Would I feel better once it was altered to my size? Was that a risk I was willing to take?

All those questions running through my mind led me to conclude that I had to, pardon the pun, trash that dress. I spent more time fretting and adding other dresses to my Pinterest planning boards than I did fantasizing about wearing the gown. I committed to a beautiful, whimsical dress, but it just wasn't the right one. The red flags were prominent.

There was no way I was going to settle. I would wait to find my perfect match of material, the dress to complement my personality and represent the woman I had become, even if it was going to take some time. Under that mindset, I found my man, so I decided the dress should now be a piece of, well, cake! I just needed to take a step back from bridezilla mode, enjoy being engaged and let the perfect dress find me.

And what do you know, it did! About five months after Frank and I got engaged, my brother and his long-time girlfriend, Jaime, decided to take the plunge. While shopping with Jaime for her wedding dress, I tried on a few that caught my eye. At first, I was frustrated because my body had changed over the years and the svelte gowns to which I was drawn didn't complement my new curves. Hello, 30s! But then, I slipped on a dress that I originally wanted but never had a chance to consider because I bought the "reject" dress.

All zipped up, I viewed my glowing face in the mirror and felt the spark. I was a bride; fitted in a clean, strapless, shantung taffeta, sweetheart gown (with pockets!) to which I planned on making minor alterations (removing the back train and a bow from the waist and adding a sash) so that it was unique. At that moment, there were no thoughts of my past wedding and I didn't compare myself to the bride I was years ago. Complete with my shrug, I could picture myself the day Frank and I booked to say our vows: October 6th.

I hate referring to my first legal commitment as a marriage. It bothers me to use the word "husband" when referring to my past, because now that I have met Frank, I know the man whose last name I once took was never worthy of that title.

I must state, my intentions have never been to portray Max as a bad person; he was just a bad choice for me as a husband. We needed each other at that time in our lives for our own selfish reasons. We both had our doubts at different points, but counted on a better outcome. That doesn't make us foolish young adults, but two people who have lived and learned.

From what I've heard, Max is doing well and I'm happy for him. He deserves harmony and success. During our breakup, he told me that he'd never forgive himself and would have to live with his actions forever. As much as I despised his choices, I'm over it.

Holding grudges only restrains progress, as any woman who has ever trashed her dress, whether metaphorically or physically, can conclude. It's important to be open to anything, get out of your comfort zone, and celebrate your brilliance! Don't waste your time bashing your ex; that will only let him get the best of you.

We're brave. We had the strength to let go and the future is our reward.

Through the process of writing this book, I realized even though I spent many nights crying about it, I never failed at *Planet Verge*. I always abided by something my favorite singer, Butch Walker, told me after one of our interviews:

"I think you always have to do what you set out in life to do, regardless of how successful you are at it. You are successful when you're doing what you want to do. You're not successful if you give up and do something you don't want to do. It's not about how much you make, as much as it is that you actually went for it."

It may not have become the best-selling magazine or Internet TV show like I aspired, but through ten plus years of sweat, financial strain and tears associated with that project, I inspired people's lives. I have fan mail from young girls across the world to remind me of that. Reflecting, my dreams actually came true in the process; just not how I planned. While chasing my professional goal, I met and fell in love with Frank.

I must say, even though I'm getting married, I still struggle with the fact that I've been divorced. Frank and I are saving for a wedding and a home of our own. It's not a carefree wedding planning process like many first-time brides experience, thanks to financial backing from their parental units. Frank and I are going to encounter obstacles along the way, but the difference this time is that we are a team. And at the end of the day, we know we'll be OK because we have each other.

One such hard time recently came out of nowhere, when this past Christmas day, we suffered the devastating loss of our dog, Skye. We pulled into our driveway on Christmas Eve and heard Skye screaming from inside the house. Walking into the house was the scariest moment of my life. I had no idea what we were going to find, but I knew it wasn't going to be a good situation. It turned out that Skye's leg was broken, twisted sideways. I was horrified. We had no idea how long she was injured, but surmised she hurt it jumping off the bed when she heard our car come home.

At the animal hospital, the vet informed us that she had bone cancer. Our only options were to amputate her leg or put her to sleep. Merry Christmas, your dog is dying.

Hysterical, I begged the doctor to let us take her home one last night and hoped to get a second opinion from our family vet in the morning. Unfortunately, our vet was vacationing in Florida and since Skye howled in agony all night, we made the most heart-breaking decision to give her peace at around 8 a.m. on Christmas morning.

Frank and I held her to the end and she kissed us both good-bye. I had been asking her all morning to give her daddy a kiss but she refused until that precious moment. The vet put her down on a Jets blanket. Maybe he saw that Frank was wearing his Jets jacket, but I like to think it was a little bit of fate intervening to show that Skye really had become Frank's dog, too.

I've never felt so much pain in my life, not even during my divorce. Skye was a member of the family. She literally brought light back into my life when I first took her home on Black Friday ten years prior. I had been depressed for months, simultaneously mourning the end of my first major relationship and the deaths of my grandmother and my golden retriever, Dusty, who had to be put down due to lymphoma. I felt alone and needed comfort. Skye became my rock.

No matter what was going on in my life, I always had her to cuddle with and put a smile on my face. We'd go for walks, chase squirrels, share snacks and make videos of her singing in that famous husky howl.

Skye's death brought a lot of emotions back into my life, particularly regret. Skye loved children and I always dreamed of giving her a baby to play alongside. But my "failed" marriage messed up those plans. I regretted that Frank and I waited to take our engagement photos and Skye would not be a part of them. I regret that the only pictures I have as a bride with Skye are from my marriage to the wrong man. I'm upset that I didn't get to dress her up for her last Christmas or give her gifts.

But if I've learned one thing from my divorce, it is that everything happens for a reason. I wasn't meant to know Skye was sick because then I would worry about her every day—and let's be honest, probably never leave the house. One night when I was sobbing so hard I could barely breathe, my mom told me that part of being a mother is doing what's best for your child. As Skye's mom, I did what was best for her and that was to let her go.

Skye may be gone, but she's still leaving her paw prints in my life. Upon hearing the news, my old best friend and maid of honor, who was one of the people I had a falling out with during my divorce, reached out and sent me an email expressing her sympathy. I was shocked but grateful to have the opportunity to make amends. We decided to put the past behind us and stay in touch. But that's not Skye's only heaven sent message.

Frank and I adopted a five-year-old plot hound mix that was ironically surrendered to a high-kill shelter on Black Friday. The shelter named her Noelle. Our rhyming names were meant to be, however we now call her Lulu (all my dogs are named after *General Hospital* characters). This little girl, a former puppy mill mom who delivered many litters and has no bottom front teeth, has helped us heal. Sometimes, the only way to accept an unwelcome turn of events is to occupy your mind with new things. Saving a life was the best way to honor the end of Skye's.

As life would have it, while dissecting my divorce and meeting all the participants for this book, I was inspired to trash my dress again. My first "trash the dress" photo shoot was a good riddance to Max. But I felt it was necessary to do one that represented optimism and would inspire young divorcées to move forward with their lives.

So, Frank and I painted the bedroom walls Tiffany blue and had an artist friend use them as her textual canvas. The words "dream," "accomplish," "hope," "love," "thrive," "celebrate," "laugh," "breathe" and "inspire" danced across the background as I cut up the remaining shreds of my first wedding gown for the shoot. I wore a silver sequin dress (partially because my reconstructed gown didn't fit me anymore!) with spiked nude heels and applied a rainbow of shadow around my eyes. The photos are bright, colorful reminders that every divorced woman should keep her spirits up because one day their dark moods will be replaced by a burst of positivity and productivity.

By celebrating divorce in my 20s, I've ripped up the old life I wrote for myself, crumbled up the pages and recycled my story. As I prepare to walk down the aisle again, I anticipate all the surprises life has in store. But one thing is for certain; this wedding dress will be preserved. And when I become Frank's wife, I'll proudly take his last name, which just so happens to translate from Italian to "hope." Ironic? I like to think it's written in the stars.

Trash the Dress
presents...
Divorceisms

They've cried.
They've conquered.
They're telling it like it is.

Trash the Dress participants share advice for women considering divorce, dating requirements for a future mate, "Good Riddance" lists, lessons learned and reasons why they're celebrating divorce.

Twenty Nine

Sister to Sister

Lean on us. There's plenty of support in the *Trash the Dress* online community, but here's some instant reassurance you made the right decision to divorce, straight from those who have been there and done that.

Alexandra from Texas wants to drill a few key points into your brain:

- "You'll have great days and you'll have bad days. On occasion, learning something about my ex-husband will open a wound and I'll be anxious and sad, and want to bring up old issues regarding our relationship. It's important to not beat yourself up for the bad days. Accept that you're still hurting and take time to re-focus on the positives."

- "Stay off of Facebook. I befriended a lot of my ex-husband's friends on Facebook during our relationship. It doesn't help the healing process to see how much fun your ex is having while you're struggling in life. So, refrain from Faceboc for a short stint!"

- "Keep a positive attitude. If you view divorcing as a flaw, that leads to other negative thoughts and it can get out of control. View divorce as a learning process and use it as an opportunity to explore yourself."

- "Don't dissect the relationship! Oh. My. God. I did this over and over again, 24 hours a day, for weeks. It doesn't help anything and is exhausting. If you've accepted that divorce is the best choice, accept that the relationship was simply not viable and leave it at that."

- "Don't compare yourself to other women who are your age and married. This exercise is pointless because we're all on our own paths, and how happiness finds us will be different."

More participants weighed in:

"My journey through my divorce was all about finding my voice and getting to know myself. I feel that when we are stuck in un-happy marriages or situations, especially when we are young, we can lose sight of who we are and what our goals are in life. And I think that finding your own way and learning to listen to your own inner voice and trusting yourself is a celebration all in itself! My best advice is to use this horrible time of our lives as a learning experience and a chance to get to know ourselves. No matter how dark the days may seem right now, there is a better life for you out there beyond the devastation of divorce."
-Kate, Connecticut

"Don't listen to anyone—only you know the situation. You are the one living your life, so don't make yourself suffer!"
-Madison, New Jersey

)on't look back, because if you do, it will be even
/ince yourself again to go through with the divorce.
ow that your friends and family love you. It doesn't
other people think of you just because you are divorced or going through one. You are just as beautiful and worthy as any other single woman out there. Being divorced is not a
big deal. It's just part of life. Think of how happy your life will be
without all these problems with your ex."
-Elizabeth, New York

"The first month is the worst. It will get better. Take ownership
for what you did but don't dwell on the why—just focus on the future. Leaving is hard. You have to make it worth it."
-Maureen, Oregon

"I know how dark and hard it seems, but this too shall pass. I often
find that saying out loud the mean things I'm thinking to myself
helps. It makes me realize that holding on to my anger isn't going
to solve things. It makes me aware of my feelings but also helps
me work through them and get to the root of the anger faster."
-Carly, New Hampshire

"It's not your fault. You're not a failure. And while it may seem
like your life is over, the next chapter is just beginning and it will
get easier with time."
-Meredith, New Jersey

"Get a lawyer. That's the most important thing. You may think
you are getting it done quickly and amicably, but you could very
easily end up screwed in this situation."
-Sydney, Florida

"Whatever doesn't kill you will only make you stronger."
-Casey, Florida

"Know that it isn't the end of the world. Life goes on, and as time passes you'll heal. You'll find someone new, someone better for you. Keep in mind that absolutely everything in life happens for a reason."
-Miranda, Wisconsin

"If the relationship is really over, let it be over. Don't be like me and keep trying and trying; it only hurts worse in the end. Just because you're divorced doesn't mean you're damaged goods. You are still a beautiful young lady with a bright future and just be glad that you got out when you did!"
-Daphne, Kentucky

"Your sisters are here on the other side and we will help you through anything."
-Liv, Pennsylvania

"Heal and love yourself. Take time to figure what's going on with you."
-Ellie, Minnesota

"Let yourself mourn, but take stock of the good things in your life. Remember how fleeting life is; don't get bogged down in misery. There is still so much time to find love and a partner, but don't let that be your only goal in life. Spend time with your family and friends. Get outdoors and take advantage of what the world has to offer. This is just a blip in the timeline of your life."
-Lily, Virginia

"Always listen to your inner voice, and don't let the opinions of others sway how you feel. Stay true to yourself and go after what makes you happy."
-Jackie, Pennsylvania

"Listen to your heart. Everyone around you is going to have an opinion but in the end you have to go do what is right for you or else you are not going to be able to be whole no matter what you choose. Everyday will be different, it's part of the rollercoaster ride of divorce. Some days you will be the captain of your best goddamn future, other days you will feel like a ruined woman. In the end you have to be OK with your choices and own them. Be strong and stand by them."
-Maxie, California

"Divorce is hard. Emotionally and physically, it takes a toll. I've never been sicker than when I was going through my divorce. I had never been to the doctor more than the year of my divorce. Things always turned out to be nothing. I had brain scans, MRIs and more! It was all stress-related. If divorce could be a medical diagnosis, I would have had it that year. Things will come at you that you couldn't have even possibly prepared yourself for during this process. Be ready to have really bad days, and embrace the good days when they show up. Don't be afraid to cry, curse and break things. And don't ever forget, you will come out on the other side of this. You are a stronger person than you give yourself credit for. And you are worthy of a better life. Now go out and grab it."
-Brooke, Wisconsin

"While I was in the midst of the emotional crisis that I experienced post-divorce, one thought kept occurring to me and provided a small level of comfort: almost 50 percent of the population go through a divorce. When I felt like I couldn't survive, when I felt like I would die from the intensity of my emotions, I thought about all of the celebrities, people I know, women, men, rich people and poor people who go through divorce. I thought about how everyone who goes through a divorce feels as hopeless, unhappy, lonely and overall miserable as I did and yet, they survived. I knew that I would too."
-Scarlett, Toronto

"The best advice I got during this time was from the woman who officiated our wedding ceremony. She said, 'The best revenge is to have a wonderful life!'"
-Leanne, New Mexico

"You are too young to settle for less than what you deserve. Every woman deserves to be treated with respect. Also, just keep in mind that you are young. A person can reinvent herself several times in her life, so take this opportunity to make yourself the woman you want to be."
-Mae, Massachusetts

"Keep your chin up and your chest out. No one ever got divorced from a good marriage. Only bad marriages end and because of that, you should be grateful for your divorce. Celebrate your divorce as a positive change for your future and a new beginning for yourself."
-Rory, Massachusetts

"Talk about it with family and friends, don't try to hold it all in. It's alright to cry and mourn, but eventually you have to realize that there is a silver lining in it all."
-Riley, Virginia

"The end of a marriage (whether by your primary choice or his) does not mean that life is over. If he chooses to end it, let that be his loss. If you choose to end it, that is your gain. No matter what, you win."
-Alice, Texas

"You are responsible for your own happiness—take it. If you are not happy with your life, change it. Don't wait around for someone or something else to change it for you. You will spend a long time in misery."
-Chloe, Texas

"You will love again. Life goes on, and this is happening for reasons that will make sense later. Breathe. Remember that you are young, and life is long."
-Harlowe, Virginia

"Learning to live as a single person again really can be just the thing you need to discover yourself in order to figure out what kind of a person you want to be with."
-Sara, Egypt

"The best is yet to come. So much of life is about how we choose to look at it. Be strong and see this as an opportunity. Take this opportunity to figure out who you are, who you want to be and carve your own path."
-Dr. Patricia Leavy, Massachusetts

"Don't think about right now, or tomorrow. Think about five years from now, because they'll be here before you know it. And then you'll be able to look back and say 'Phew! I'm glad that's over! I survived, and I'm OK.'"
-Caroline, Nevada

"Stay strong. You got to this point for a reason so don't allow him back because he says he'll change. Men (and women) never change."
-Rachel, Maryland

"Be strong and be on your own. Never rely on anyone."
-Hannah, North Carolina

"Always follow your heart. I know it sounds cliché. But at some point in your life you have to worry about your own happiness. You have to stop caring what other people think. You have to be a little 'selfish.' And sometimes when it seems like the darkest time of your life it's only because you're covering your own

eyes, ignoring what you know is right. Currently, I am the happiest woman in the world. I am blessed more than anyone could be. There is a light at the end of the tunnel. You just have to be strong enough to make it out."
-Clara, New Jersey

Thirty

Check, Mate

After marriage, participants found out what's really important in a partner. Let's learn from each other's misfortunes.

Here's what should be on your dating checklist:

"The main thing is that I want someone who likes me for me. I am OK with compromise, but not to the point that I start to act differently, as if my personality is slightly altered. I also want someone who will tell me how they feel about me, tell me they love me and that I look beautiful, and really mean it. Also, punctuality is important! I can't wait for a man anymore; I've done enough of that to last a lifetime."
-Lily, Virginia

"There has to be good sex! I was raised by a strict Catholic mom who made us think sex was dirty and women weren't supposed to enjoy it. I realize now that sex is important—it makes you feel bonded to someone and I won't have a sexless relationship again."
-Maureen, Oregon

"Someone who is athletic (or tries to be, all I want is effort), willing to try new foods, and likes animals."
-Hadley, New York

"He must love cats. Must be motivated and someone who dreams big and in color."
-Carly, New Hampshire

"He must not be an addict or in recovery and he must have good credit, a college degree, a home and take good care of himself."
-Fiona, Maryland

"Someone who is open to traveling and seeing the world and experiencing new cultures and ideas. They also have to accept my dogs as part of the family. Treating me with respect is also important. I spent too long being verbally disrespected and I don't want to tolerate that anymore. I also appreciate sensitivity and passion in a mate; someone who isn't afraid to show emotion and encourages me to do the same. I was very emotionally stifled by my soon-to-be ex, who would often tell me I was 'being ridiculous and crazy' when I was emotional."
-Jackie, Pennsylvania

"A sense of humor. This is so important. My ex-husband and I had such different senses of humor we were on different pages. Also, someone who is ambitious and educated. I already have a master's and am working on another bachelor's degree and subsequent master's. I can't be with someone who only did a few semesters."
-Maxie, California

"A caring and compassionate person, who puts others before himself. A person who makes love a priority, and the object of their love a priority. Intelligence, and I don't mean book learning necessarily. A man with a wonderful family that he loves and that I can

love as much as I love my own family. Someone I can laugh with and that I can play with."
-Brooke, Wisconsin

"Appreciation for the arts."
-Leanne, New Mexico

"Not addicted to porn."
-Mae, Massachusetts

"He has to be my intellectual equal. Someone with whom I can have stimulating conversations. I want to find someone very similar to myself, who is passionate about the same things and wants the same type of lifestyle."
-Juniper, Oklahoma

"Must be willing to go to church with me and be involved with life there. Must want children. Must be a nice person—no yelling at people in public. This includes traffic. Must know how to do his laundry. I'm his wife not his mama."
-Chloe, Texas

"He must know how to talk about problems. He must be willing to listen and communicate, and not sweep everything under the rug. And he must be someone I feel is my best friend, and vice versa."
-Harper, Arizona

"My number one must-have quality is the ability to be independent. I can no longer take care of my husband—no lost puppies allowed. Another must-have quality is the ability to appreciate things that people do for you in life and want to make your significant other happy and have concern for their needs."
-Jezabelle, New York

"He's got to be a friend first before anything else."
-Sara, Egypt

"My next marriage must be an equal partnership. I want a man to share my faith but be theologically flexible and open. He should be comfortable with sexuality—experimental and fun in bed and not uncomfortable around sexual innuendo. I need someone who is supportive but in a way that respects my process and who I am, rather than having some preset agenda for me. He should share enough of my interests where we have many things we like to do and talk about together. And he must love my dog. Oh, and I want us to laugh together a lot."
-Grace, Pennsylvania

"Someone who is non-material, down to earth and sexually active."
-Violet, Australia

Thirty One

Good Riddance!

What's behind a young divorcée's smile? For these participants, it's the fact that they no longer have to deal with the
pet peeves that accompanied marriage. You know, like their ex's
farting, laziness and lack of employment.

Read some of their "good riddances" and make a "warning" list
of your own.

"He used olive oil instead of gel on his hair, smelled like garlic and
had gross teeth."
-Carly, New Hampshire

"His obsession with being in the 'Mile High Club' and feeling me
up on planes when I wasn't interested."
-Alice, Texas

"When he shaved or cut his hair, my bathroom was always a mess."
-Daphne, Kentucky

"He would leave food out to rot."
-Liv, Pennsylvania

"Chewing tobacco... eww!"
-Kensie, Minnesota

"For Valentine's Day one year he bought himself a TV and $2,000 boxing match tickets for a trip he kept a secret. I'm a teacher and kids will get me gifts for the occasion so he said he didn't have to get me anything."
-Fiona, Maryland

"We went to France on a two-week trip a few years ago. We spent almost all of our savings and used almost all of our work vacation time, so it was a huge deal. He spent the better part of the trip doing work on his phone. He had people who were dealing with his clients while he was away, so there was no reason whatsoever that he needed to be on his phone at all. It was just another way in which our marriage was a low priority in his life. His bill that month ended up being about $1,000."
-Lily, Virginia

"His ability to manipulate me and always make me feel like any conflicts we had were my fault, and that I was crazy or unreasonable. He created so much self-doubt in my head that I always questioned myself and believed that maybe he was right. I spent most of our relationship apologizing for things that were absolutely not my fault."
-Jackie, Pennsylvania

"He was filthy. Seriously, the man didn't shower. He smelled. And he dressed like my grandfather."
-Brooke, Wisconsin

"His beer gut that he never seemed to keep off, farting, and needing to pick his nose and every zit he ever got."
-Rory, Massachusetts

"I hated that he wasn't interested in any of my projects or things I cared about."
-Juniper, Oklahoma

"The way he left his dirty boxer briefs on the bathroom floor for me to pick up."
-Riley, Virginia

"He didn't do anything around the house. If he did it was supposed to be celebrated with much fanfare. Did I get any fanfare for cooking or cleaning? Nope. I also mowed the grass more than he did. We bought a house with an above ground pool and he said he could get it working. It sat stagnant for almost three years. I'm the one who ended up cleaning it and getting it working—after he left."
-Chloe, Texas

"He wore these damn corduroy pants and cut-off jean shorts that were so atrocious. And he wore socks to bed."
-Cherie, California

"His insane obsession with state sports."
-Harlowe, Virginia

"He was so damn cheap it killed me."
-Sara, Eqypt

"He always insisted he was right."
-Caroline, Nevada

"He was selfish, narcissistic, disloyal, and manipulative... but on a more petty level he never shut doors or drawers, would take off his undershirt and shirts together so when I did laundry there was always the shirt inside the shirt that belonged in two different loads, and his car was always filthy."
-Molly, Massachusetts

"He bit his nails and flicked them on the couch."
-Grace, Pennsylvania

Thirty Two

Lessons Learned

Everything happens for a reason. Here's what twenty-something divorcées have learned about life, love, and themselves. Soak in their wisdom from wifedom and beyond:

"I have watched my life and the plan I had for my life crumble before my eyes and somehow I survived. I have watched my ex-husband buy a house when I am stuck in our old apartment. I watched him get remarried and continue his life barely skipping a beat. I have heard the news that his new wife is having a baby and giving my child the sibling that I cannot give to him right now, and somehow I have survived. I was the girl who thought she couldn't manage to live another day after my ex moved out, but I stand here alive and well and I did all this while working full-time, going to school to further my career, raising a young child, and beating a life-threatening eating disorder that held me captive for so long. It taught me to lean on my family and trust them to help me and guide me. It actually brought me closer than ever to my family—these relationships had been somewhat neglected for a long time."
-Kate, Connecticut

"I learned that I am a strong woman. That I'm not weak, that nobody can ever do this to me again. I learned that there are other great guys out there that do like me and don't mind my history. And I won't take any more crap from anyone!"
-Elizabeth, New York

"I learned that I put way too much stock into what other people think of me and that's how I get myself into bad situations. That I don't give up on people quickly enough. That it's OK to put myself first."
-Maureen, Oregon

"I learned that I am way more badass than I ever imagined. I actually sort of like my sassy self. She'd been hidden for way too long. Also, I will never compromise myself for a man ever again. If he can't handle me as I am, I don't want him. And I don't need a man. For a while I believed I needed him. Now I see how completely ridiculous that sentiment was! Also, I learned that weddings don't make marriages, and I think too many people place too much emphasis on the wedding rather than the marriage. If I get married again I want the marriage experience, not the wedding experience."
-Carly, New Hampshire

"Opposites may attract, but long term, they repel!"
-Maisie, Missouri

"Trust your gut instincts and look out for number one."
-Casey, Florida

"Date someone for at least two years before getting married. Know almost everything about my partner before getting married and keep my eyes open as to his history. Recognize there are always two sides to the story and things may not always be as they seem. Accept that a person is who they are when I meet them. They won't change! Have the courage to end the

relationship if I see it's harmful for me. Be honest with myself in how I feel about my partner. Maintain my own separate life and not become dependent on my partner! When I was married, my ex-husband and I had so much going on, that I only wanted to spend time with him when we had 'alone time.' Because of that, I secluded myself and didn't focus on maintaining my friendships."
-Alexandra, Texas

"I could have worked my butt off and done everything to try to make that marriage work but at the end of the day, marriage is two-sided. I didn't fail at anything."
-Liz, Massachusetts

"I can't lie about who I am and what I want, and if someone doesn't love me for everything I am, and all my flaws, then it won't work and we are not meant to be."
-Liv, Pennsylvania

"I learned to take care of myself and make sure I wasn't getting into a relationship for the money and support."
-Ellie, Minnesota

"I learned that I really need to work on being happy with myself. That's the only way that I can be happy with my relationship, career, everything!"
-Mindi, Pennsylvania

"Don't get married until you already feel married and it's happy and healthy."
-Kensie, Minnesota

"You can't force someone to be the person you want them to be. You cannot push your own morals and values on someone. Don't

be so desperate to start the next chapter in your life, enjoy the chapter you are in."
-Fiona, Maryland

"I learned that you can't please everyone, and there will always be some people who disagree with your life decisions. Sometimes you have to stand up for what you feel is right for yourself and not be swayed by the expectations of others."
-Jackie, Pennsylvania

"Kill the timeline. Just live life."
-Brooke, Wisconsin

"Emotional abuse is hard to pinpoint, but it is very, very real. And I probably wouldn't be so adamant about it if I hadn't seen it, heard it and felt it for myself. I hope that I have learned to recognize it if it ever shows its ugly face to me again. It led me into such a deep depression, that I didn't even recognize myself anymore. I gained weight, felt like I wasn't good enough, lost interest in things I loved, and drank a lot more than I probably should have."
-Mae, Massachusetts

"I've learned that I made mistakes that got me to where I am now, but I don't have to suffer for the rest of my life because of them. I can learn from them and move on happier, wiser and better."
-Rory, Massachusetts

"Sometimes the bad lets us appreciate the good."
-Lucy, Texas

"I just know now, that soul mates exist. I know now that I can live on my own."
-Justine, New York

"If I had been honest and open with myself from the very beginning, I would never have gotten married."
-Juniper, Oklahoma

"Never settle for anything less than you deserve."
-Riley, Virginia

"I learned that being married can be the loneliest thing in the world. And that developing your own character first is the true foundation for developing a real relationship with a life partner. It's possible to go through life superficially married to someone and without ever finding out who you really are."
-Monica, Hong Kong

"I can't control everything. Life is one big adventure and it's meant to just be taken one day at a time because you never know when everything can change."
-Emily, North Carolina

"Always get divorce stuff in writing, through the courts. This helps in case you need it years later."
-Harper, Arizona

"Loving someone isn't enough. Just because I love someone so endlessly and unconditionally does not mean that they love me the same way."
-Cherie, California

"I don't need to search for someone to make me happy. I am the only one who can make me happy."
-Jezzabelle, New York

"Life goes on. Life is long and even when things feel like they are the end of the world, they are just small pieces in the grand

scheme of things. Divorce is shitty, but so is staying in a shitty marriage."
-Harlowe, Virginia

"The romantic comedy image of marriage and relationships is just not accurate. It's OK to love watching those stories, but measuring your life to that image is trouble and expecting that image will disappoint."
-Nora, North Carolina

"Never rush anything, do not crack under pressure, and listen to your friends!"
-Sara, Egypt

"I realized that you cannot change a man and that I don't need a man. Also, if it feels wrong or if you break up, then break up for good, do not go back."
-Rachel, Maryland

"Pain is just weakness leaving the body."
-Molly, Massachusetts

"I've learned to live much more in the present. I had to learn that you can't change anyone but yourself and I've learned a lot about letting go."
-Kelly, New York

"To get respect from someone you have to communicate it and demand it. You control how you get treated. Always keep a broad perspective and don't focus on your fears. Keep rational!"
-Violet, Australia

"Marry within your religion or level of spirituality. I never thought I'd speak those words since I'm not religious and open to

everything, but when in love, you're seeing things through rose-colored glasses. The religion conversation will ultimately come up when you're planning a family. Neither of us wanted to lose that part of our identity, and we decided that we shouldn't have to."
-Penny, New Jersey

Thirty Three

Happily Ever After Divorce

"**D**ivorce" is a beautiful word. It represents rebirth, knowledge, freedom and opportunity. Whenever life gets you down, just turn to this page of "divorceisms" to remind yourself why the end of your marriage just may be the best thing to ever happen in your life thus far.

"Although I sometimes hate to admit it and my past mistakes, divorce saved my life. It has given me a second chance."
-Kate, Connecticut

"I made a mistake, and I can fix it, and start over with a whole new approach to life."
-Hadley, New York

"I feel stripped down—like everyone has seen all of my dirty laundry, but it's still OK. You realize that none of that matters; it's all artificial."
-Maureen, Oregon

"No one controls me now, no one dictates who I see, when I see them, and how much money I spend. If I want a $300 dress or pair of shoes, I buy them. I may regret my credit card bill, but I don't have anyone behind me belittling my choices."
-Carly, New Hampshire

"Divorce gave me my life back. I felt I had given up my existence; lost the essence of who I am. Getting a divorce gave me a permission slip to pursue life. I didn't feel like I lost; I felt like I won. I'm a champion."
-Bethany, Ohio

"I have to say, other than the birth of my daughter, this was the best thing I have experienced. The experience was pure, unforgiving hell, but I learned. I matured, I grew spiritually, I gained a new perspective on life, I discovered issues that I had never addressed, and I accepted who I was. I learned what love is, what love is not, what I value in a marriage and relationship, what kind of man will compliment me, and how to function in a healthy relationship."
-Alexandra, Texas

"I found the young, beautiful 16-year-old girl that I loved that I had left behind."
-Daphne, Kentucky

"I feel like a film has been lifted from my eyes, and I can genuinely enjoy and appreciate my life in a way I have never done before. In relation to love, I may not believe in the fallacy that there is one right person for everyone, but I do believe love is out there and that I have been offered an opportunity to get it right eventually. I will not be laboring under any false ideals of love now. I have experienced it at its worst and at its best. I know it takes hard work, but I also think it should feel easy. But most importantly, I now know that allowing myself

independence is what will help me find true togetherness with someone someday. I am learning more about what I like, hate and deserve with each moment that passes. Every day I thank my ex-husband for affording me the opportunity to realize that."
-Lily, Virginia

"I have been given the opportunity to rewrite my future. There are endless possibilities from here on out because now I can be 'selfish.' Every single one of my friends in a serious relationship or married happily or not has come up to me and told me that they are jealous of me because I'm my own free agent now."
-Maxie, California

"If divorce leaves a scar, I proudly wear it for all to see—because it did me a favor. It got me out of a sad, sour life, and it got me into a limitless land of love and possibilities."
-Brooke, Wisconsin

"This divorce was the best thing that ever happened to me because it showed me the people in my life that were always going to be there, and that I do not ever want to be far away from them again."
-Mae, Massachusetts

"I think that sometimes, 'intact' homes can be the most broken and divorce saved my son and me from that."
-Rory, Massachusetts

"By making my own choices and striking out on my own, I communicated the fact that I was grown and no one was going to force me to live the life they thought was best for me. Before my divorce, I didn't have the courage or the will to stand up to my family or anyone else. Getting divorced was my rebirth."
-Juniper, Oklahoma

"It made me become an individual and not just half of a marriage. I can now define myself much more clearly."
-Nora, North Carolina

"Divorce. I used to think it was such a terrible word. But now to me divorce is my new beginning. I've been given a chance to start over and have been granted the wisdom to learn from my mistakes."
-Sara, Egypt

It's Your Time To...

C elebrate, cry, laugh, smash that vase you received as a bridal shower gift, burn your wedding photos, accomplish goals, BREATHE, inspire others, kiss strangers, cash in your life savings and go backpacking through Europe, buy sexy new lingerie, finally learn how to cook, write a good riddance list, juggle multiple men, adopt the puppy you've always wanted, learn a new language, sell your wedding ring, host a divorce party, buy a voo doo doll and tape on a photo of your ex-husband, make a dating checklist, start something, take a bubble bath every night, get a tarot card reading, hit the road with your girlfriends, indulge in monthly facials, chop your hair, run a marathon, do a pin-up style photo shoot, give yourself a brand new last name, start a blog, vent to a therapist, sing karaoke, dance like no one is watching, accept every invitation, begin a vegan diet, secretly sign up for an online dating site, get a tattoo, form a band, practice yoga, go back to college, start your own company, fall in love again, have fun with no remorse, live your life for yourself, take a sick day, sprawl out in the middle of the bed, paint your walls pink, shine, go for it. Now. **Trash the dress. Live your dream.**

Update

Hello, future.

It's been about three years since I began interviewing participants for this book and two years since I completed the manuscript draft. What have I been doing in between, you ask? Playing the waiting game.

It's been incredibly hard to give up control of my "baby" and rely on those in the corporate world to get this book published. There are not enough young divorced women out there to purchase this book, or so they told me. Add a professional expert as a co-author to examine its contents, they suggested. No, thank you.

I didn't write this book so publishers or agents could profit from its sales. And adding a professional expert as a co-author defeats the whole purpose of this book, which is to tell the stories of real women going through divorce in their 20s. There are enough books from professionals out there. We don't need another one of those books on shelves. Society needs to hear from the *real* young divorce experts. I'm talking about the women who shared their journeys with me.

I wrote this book to inspire the young women whose shoes I was once wearing. I wrote it for young divorcées only. And I'm going to find them and ensure they have this in their hands when they are in their beds crying because their lives are falling apart. I am going to make sure they know they are not alone, that there is a worldwide group of women who have already found *Trash the*

Dress online, to support them. I've always been a DIY-er and if I can't rely on the reach of big publishing houses to get the word out to the masses, then I'm going to do it myself, little by little until I reach every twenty-something divorcée in need.

It's crazy. When I first started this endeavor, I was worried about finding five girls to participate. Now, I've met hundreds (and I hope we grow to thousands because I know there are more young divorcées out there!) of amazing women through my blog at www.TrashTheDressOnline.com and our private Facebook support group. Each girl inspires me daily. I'm so proud of everyone's accomplishments and have loved watching the group members accomplish their dreams, earn Ph.D.s, buy houses on their own, be rock star single moms, take solo trips, venture out on dates, fall in love, get engaged and married, and have babies. We're living the futures we agonized over and it turns out we made it! And we're doing more than alright.

As I type this, I'm sitting in the office of a little red ranch house Frank and I purchased right before we got married. My favorite album is playing. As I decide what I want to type next, I rest my hand on my growing belly. I'm nine months pregnant with a baby girl, who we will name Genevieve. Everything I ever wanted is finally happening.

It took five years post-divorce in my 20s (so be patient, ladies!) but I am finally where I've always wanted to be. Frank and I had a beautiful rustic-inspired wedding that made me cry. If you recall, it was during the ceremony to my ex-husband, that I realized I was making a mistake. I didn't feel any emotion as I said my vows. This time, things were quite the opposite.

I cried during our "first look" pictures. We decided to see each other in private before the ceremony. As I walked towards Frank, who had his back to me, I was suddenly flooded with nervous excitement and started weeping as soon as he turned around. I tried to contain myself in an effort to save my makeup but it didn't work. I experienced the feeling I yearned for the first time I got married and missed throughout that entire marriage.

Minutes later, Frank and I walked down the aisle together to say our vows. Our wedding symbolized each of us overcoming our past and building a much-deserved happy life together, so it was only fitting. Despite a limited budget, we were able to host a beautiful event and celebrate with family and close friends.

We thought we'd never be able to afford a wedding and a house, but somehow, we made it happen. And now, we're starting our family. I still can't believe that I'm pregnant. I am so excited to meet our little girl and be her mommy. I know our fur-children will adore her, too!

I actually confirmed my pregnancy the day before Christmas Eve. It was the first anniversary of saying goodbye to Skye and I told Frank that we needed something to make Christmas a happy occasion again. I believe this baby was Skye's gift.

I'm now 33, years away from my divorce and even farther from my teenage dream of being a wife and mother by age 26, but I know this is the way my life was supposed to play out.

I'm so grateful for divorce in my 20s because it brought me to have the life I always wanted in my 30s. Looking back, I wouldn't change a thing. I'm finally at a place where I feel at peace. I know that not everything will be easy, but I've always remained faithful and it's always gotten me to where I can thrive. The hard times were so worth going through because these good times ahead are going to be the best times.

As for my ex-husband? He actually sent me a text message a few months after I remarried. A mutual acquaintance had informed him of my marriage and Skye's passing. He said that even though we don't talk anymore, he wanted to wish me the best of luck. Then, he expressed his condolences, confessing that because of Skye and me, he became a dog lover and that she and Lucky will always have a special place in his heart.

I was surprised and cordially responded. There's no need for us to further communicate, but I appreciate the courage it took for him to reach out. It shows he has moved on with his life as well. We weren't meant to be married, but maybe it all happened because I was meant to convert one more person into a dog lover. What a journey I had to endure for that!

In all seriousness, I hope this book has helped everyone reading it as much as it helped me to write it. I'm always told how grateful everyone is that I formed this project. I'm equally indebted to everyone for participating! We have become a sisterhood of young divorcées. We're really an international family, helping each other along our journeys. And if we're lucky, those of us who live near each other get to become real life friends, like Ariel and I.

Remember how stressed out Ariel was about not having any children when she divorced? She remarried one month after me and is also nine months pregnant—with a baby boy! We realized we live about 20 minutes from each other and now double date.

Here's to happy endings, new beginnings and friendships that wouldn't have been formed without our divorces! More proof that everything happens for a reason—in due time!

Acknowledgement

My book team:

PHOTOGRAPHY: Jenna Przybylowski (Jenna Zee). You're there to capture all the stages of my life. The front and back covers of this book would not be as eye-catching as they are without your photography from my second "trash the dress" photo shoot.

ART: Jessica Lynn Day. Thank you for bringing my vision to life and for creating an awesome backdrop for my second "trash the dress" photo shoot (as pictured on back cover). I wish I could have taken my old bedroom walls and all the inspiring words you painted on them with me when I moved.

COPYEDITING: Kate Fresso. Em Dash! I will never forget this symbol. Ever. Thank you for spending your summer copyediting my manuscript. And standing in line for hours with me during *Beverly Hills, 90210* cast member book signings. I obviously married into the right family!

PEACE OF MIND: Ashley Hill. Thank you for always answering my legal questions!

To those who have supported me as I chased this dream:

My family: Thank you for helping me get back on my feet and always being there. As annoyed as I would get whenever you asked me for updates on this book, I know it's because you care. I would not be where I am today without you.

Frank: It takes a special man to be in a relationship with a woman who is always writing about her first marriage and subsequent divorce and an even bigger man to proofread pages for her. You may not have been the first chapter of my life, but you are my last. I'm so very lucky to have you for a husband and to be able to grow our family together. I can't wait to see what the future has in store for us.

Genevieve: You are my dream come true. Though you are only 25 days old as I edit this section, you have inspired me the entire time I wrote this book. My end goal has always been to be happily married with a baby. Having a beautiful little girl is a bonus. Every time I look into your eyes, tears swell mine. Daddy and I are so in love with you and look forward to watching you grow up. We are truly blessed.

"Penny": We've been through it all together and it's crazy how our lives mirror each other's. I cherish our coffee-fueled conversations, the most notable of which inspired me to write this book!

Jessica S.: Thanks for standing up for me on social media when sneaky reporters publish my quotes out of context. And of course, Frank and I thank you for getting ordained to officiate our wedding!

"Molly": You stepped up and supported me through my divorce when many others judged me and I'll never forget that.

Nicole and Megan: Talented and jobless. Best summer ever. My, how much our lives have changed since then. I'm glad we went through those times together.

Trash the Dress: Stories of Celebrating Divorce in your 20s

To every young divorced woman and *Trash the Dress* member out there: This is for you.

For every participant who shared her story with me: This book would not have been possible without you! Thank you for coming forward, being honest about your experiences and opening up old wounds to help heal others.

To everyone reading this: Please don't tell me if you find any typos. I'm literally approving final edits after sleepless nights with a newborn!

To all the critics out there who are going to judge the contents of this book and publish their negative commentary on young divorce: We don't care what you say. This book is not for you.

Please forgive me if I forgot anyone directly. I appreciate all of the love and support that has come my way.

Stay in touch with me at www.TrashTheDressBook.com and www.TrashTheDressOnline.com.

The book may have ended, but the inspiring stories continue!

About the Author

Photographer: Jenna Przybylowski

Joelle Caputa is a writer, editor and public relations maven. She founded an all-female staffed 'zine that transitioned into a popular indie lifestyle website and Internet TV channel, reporting on "what's hot and what's important." During that time, she produced, hosted, and edited segments with international superstars, including Thirty Seconds to Mars and David Garrett, stood whiskers away from endangered tigers while reporting on their plight, and organized events to benefit shelter dogs.

Her articles have been published on *The Huffington Post* (her post "Why Women in their 20s Get Hitched When They Should've Ditched" was named one of the top 12 Blog Posts that Sparked Debate in 2011), *The Nest, Teen People, Venus 'Zine* and in other media outlets.

As a PR pro, her portfolio boasts a decorated and diverse array of clips. She has landed her clients on MTV (*Jersey Shore, The Real World*), Showtime, AOL Radio, in *The New York Times, The Wall Street Journal,* and *Forbes.*

Her book, *Trash the Dress: Stories of Celebrating Divorce in your 20s,* has been featured globally in The International Business Times, The Sydney Morning Herald (Australia), Maclean's (Canada), The Globe and Mail (Canada) and on Dr. Oz's YouBeauty.com, to name a few.

She lives in New Jersey in a stylish converted log cabin with her husband and brand new daughter and their two rescue pups.

Made in the USA
Middletown, DE
28 July 2015